Wiring Up The
Big Brother Machine...
And Fighting It

Wiring Up The Big Brother Machine... And Fighting It

By Mark Klein

Foreword by James Bamford

BookSurge

ISBN-10   1-4392-2996-1
ISBN-13   978-1-4392-2996-5

Library of Congress Control Number: 2009902276

Cover photo by Mark Klein of door to secret room 641A
taken in 2004 from inside AT&T's 4ESS switchroom
at 611 Folsom St., San Francisco, California
(full image on page 27)

BookSurge
7290 B Investment Drive
Charleston, South Carolina 29418
www.BookSurge.com

Printed in the United States of America

Dedicated to

Dismantling Big Brother

Contents

Acknowledgments

IT IS NOT AN EXAGGERATION to say this book would not have happened without my wife, Linda Klein, who gave me much needed support and reassurance at a scary time when I could confide in no one else. She is my life companion and the love of my life. Fortuitously, when it came time to produce this book, she was able to draw on her experience in book production to help me bring this into being.

When I started shopping for a publisher I could not find a willing candidate—I was, after all, not the typical "Washington insider" who leaves the administration with a fat book deal in hand. The big publishers never called me, and the smaller independents I canvassed were almost totally uninterested. The only offer came with an unacceptable requirement to cut core material. So I decided to self-publish my book, and that was feasible only because of Linda.

I thank Peter Goodman of Stone Bridge Press who gave me valuable advice about the publishing business.

My gratitude goes to the Playboy Foundation for naming me a winner of the 2008 Hugh M. Hefner First Amendment Award, which came with a decent sum of money that I used to cover the cost of publishing this book. Thank you Christie Hefner for your support.

When journalists James Risen and Eric Lichtblau published their revelations about the government's warrantless spying in the *New York Times* in December 2005, they coincidentally wedged the door open for me, so I'd like to say thanks for that.

I pay tribute to the Electronic Frontier Foundation, a wonderful group of energetic, enthusiastic people who really believe in defending the democratic principles embedded in the U.S. Constitution. I was all alone when I tried at first to go public in January 2006, and so I was greatly relieved when their Executive Director Shari Steele welcomed me into their office and quickly introduced me to Senior Staff Attorneys Lee Tien and Kevin Bankston, who made it clear that they wanted to examine the material I offered them about AT&T's illegal collaboration with the NSA. When they told me they were already preparing a lawsuit against the company, I knew I was in the right place, and I became a witness in the lawsuit.

I particularly enjoyed working with EFF's Legal Director Cindy Cohn and Kevin Bankston in our joint campaign to lobby Washington in late 2007. Though we failed to stop Congress's retroactive immunity for the telecoms, the effort was a useful revelation about the sleazy workings of Washington, which became an integral part of my book. Special thanks goes to Designer/Activist Hugh D'Andrade of EFF, who designed the delightful cartoon of "Mr. Klein Goes to Washington," as well as the useful graphic of the splitter apparatus, and gave me permission to use both without royalty requirements.

I am deeply indebted to my personal attorneys, James Brosnahan and Tony West of Morrison & Foerster LLP , and Miles Ehrlich and Ismail "Izzy" Ramsey of Ramsey & Ehrlich LLP. In hindsight, I must have been in great danger when I started going public in early 2006 without any legal counsel at all, and just in the nick of time I was referred to Miles and

Izzy, who started giving me excellent legal protection. When the big guns of AT&T started aiming at me, I was thankful that Jim and Tony came in to help, and they stuck with me all the way, effectively covering me against whatever the company and the government may have been contemplating.

I owe James Bamford a note of thanks for taking the time to write a foreword to my book. He is the leading public expert on the NSA in this country and it is an honor that he contributed here. In fact his original groundbreaking book about the NSA, *The Puzzle Palace* (1982), popped into my mind years later when I found the spy apparatus at AT&T, and helped me put two-and-two together. His latest book, *The Shadow Factory* (2008), adds greatly to our knowledge of the NSA's spreading tentacles in the Bush years.

Much appreciation goes to the folks at Wired.com, who persuaded their corporate owners at Condé Nast to allow me to reprint excerpts of some of their articles, particularly those by Kevin Poulsen, Ryan Singel, David Kravets, and Editor-in-Chief Evan Hansen. Wired.com played a crucial role in this story by daring to post the AT&T documents and my analysis of them on May 17, 2006, at a time when that material was still under court seal. Thus they provided a crucial public service of bringing it all out into the public domain, so all can see what the government has done. They are truly courageous journalists.

I want to send my best wishes to all the technicians I worked with at AT&T, particularly in the last couple of years at the former Geary St. office and 611 Folsom St. where the NSA showed up. It was a pleasure to work with them, and I'm sure they understand why I was not in contact with them in recent years. Special thanks goes to my former manager Don Henry, who had the wonderful combination of infinite patience, incorruptible honesty and a talent for bringing out the best in people so they can work together. I was grateful that he corroborated part of my story in his brief appearance on PBS's *Frontline* in 2007.

A final note of thanks goes to photographer Quinn Norton for the courtesy of allowing me to reprint gratis his great photos of me and my attorneys on the steps of the San Francisco courthouse.

Foreword

By James Bamford

ON A TYPICAL DAY, 210 billion e-mail messages travel around the globe—two million a second. And in the U.S. alone on that typical day, Americans talk on the phone over five and a half billion minutes and send more than one and a half billon text messages. Much of that communication enters the United States unceremoniously a few feet beneath a sandy beach at California's Montaña de Oro State Park, near Morro Bay. Despite its quiet surroundings, it is a very busy place. Five of the six transpacific cables pass under that sand, cables containing 80 percent of all communications to and from virtually every nation in the Pacific and the Far East. From Morro Bay, much of that communication travels to a massive, nine-story windowless building in downtown San Francisco, AT&T's "switch" for much of the western part of the country.

Passing into that switch at the speed of light are cries and laughter, hopes and dreams, romance and commerce, voices and pictures, e-mail and faxes, bank statements and hotel reservations, love poems and death notices. Sealed in thick polyethylene and steel fiber-optic cables and protected by law from tampering, the only thing they all have in common is a reasonable expectation of privacy.

That expectation, however, was suddenly shattered when a longtime AT&T technician noticed an odd door in the building, a door to a room for which there was no key and in which no one was allowed to enter—a secret room. Mark Klein's discovery of that room led him on a long and courageous investigation for answers—answers that shocked Americans and led to secret debates from Capitol Hill to the White House.

What he found was that the communications on those cables were secretly copied and then sent one floor below directly to the NSA's secret room. There, according to documents Klein was able to obtain, hardware and software supplied by a private company was able to search through the billions of messages at lightning speed and select out NSA's targets—targets for which the agency never obtained a warrant. Once selected out, the messages were then forwarded on to agency analysts thousands of miles away. Today, the NSA's watchlist is over half a million names long.

Mark Klein's discovery of that room, and his courageous investigation and fight for answers, is a milestone in understanding how the National Security Agency, America's largest and most secret intelligence organization, was able to spend years conducting illegal warrantless eavesdropping.

His work generated an unprecedented lawsuit that challenged the right of the government to secretly place electronic filters on the massive electronic pipes through which all of our most private communications flow. But that suit, by the Electronic Frontier Foundation against AT&T, was considered so threatening to the secrecy of the company's collaboration with NSA that the Bush White House invoked the rarely used state secrets privilege and Congress took the unprecedented step of ordering it stopped. As a result, much of what NSA did, and continues to do, remains sealed away in that secret room and in the agency's cyber-locked offices at Ft. Meade.

Now in his book Mark Klein has the chance to tell his remarkable story, a story of courage and frustration, of privacy and secrecy, and of right and wrong. As someone who has written three books on the NSA and taken part in another lawsuit to stop the agency's warrantless spying, one valiantly fought by the ACLU, I know some of what he went up against and I have great admiration for his decision to take on that battle.

James Bamford
June 1, 2009

JAMES BAMFORD is the leading public expert on the NSA and the author of the groundbreaking book *The Puzzle Palace* (1982), and more recently *Body of Secrets: Anatomy of the Ultra-Secret National Security Agency* (2002), and bestselling *The Shadow Factory* (2008).

FIGHTING BIG BROTHER

Chapter 1

Working at AT&T

In 1981, the year I was hired at AT&T, the company was an icon of America alongside GM, IBM and other blue chip companies. "Ma Bell" was a historic legal monopoly which had wired America with the telephone for a century, and it had a well-earned reputation which combined technological know-how with paternalistic anti-unionism.

The company's longtime main union, the Communications Workers of America (CWA), originated in the 1930s as a literal company union which evolved into one that was forced to actually lead strikes for better pay, benefits, and just plain respect from the arrogant management. Perhaps no one depicted the flavor of the company culture better than Lily Tomlin in her satirical 1970s Rowan & Martin *Laugh-In* skits of telephone operator Ernestine who sneered at the public with a snort, "We don't care, we don't have to—We're the Phone Company!" In truth, the mostly female operators were among the most downtrodden employees, but the skits captured the attitude of management.

I was lucky to be hired in one of the last major hiring waves at AT&T. Two forces were coming together to squeeze the workforce for the next two decades: the microchip/computer revolution and an across-the-board anti-union offensive. The spreading technological revolution gave the company the tools to automate away tens of thousands of jobs, while the unions' retreat and failure to fight back demoralized the workforce.

This process was exacerbated by the court-ordered breakup ("divestiture") of the company in 1984, which spun off pieces into seven regional companies, and more spin-offs came in the following years. The CWA led two nation-wide strikes in 1983 and 1986, in which I participated, to establish its contract terms for all the companies in the ensuing period, but the union's decline at AT&T accelerated when it abandoned the strike weapon in the 1990s.

The post-divestiture AT&T had 365,000 employees in 1985, one-third of them management, while the CWA boasted a membership of over 125,000 spread across the country. By 2005, the year after I retired, union membership was a shadow of its former self at a mere 12,000[1] and was still plunging. The remaining workers were living in sheer terror, constantly worried about losing their jobs, and the once-mighty management was arranging to have the company bought out by one of the "Baby Bells," SBC, which renamed itself "at&t."

I was originally hired in New York City into the union position of Communications Technician because I had a background in electronics and computers. My technical training included certificates from the RCA Institute of Electronics and the then-popular Control Data Institute, after which I spent a few years working in electronics/computer factories in California, including Singer/Friden and Diablo Systems, inventor of the daisywheel printer. All these companies eventually went under, victims of not only technological change, but also ruthless corporate warfare and industrial decline in the U.S.

Because of my background, I was hired directly into a

---

1. IBEW News, "CWA, IBEW and AT&T Begin Negotiations," Nov. 2, 2005. Fewer than a thousand of the remaining union workers belonged to the International Brotherhood of Electrical Workers.

computer room at 33 Thomas St. in Manhattan, and thus by-passed the traditional entry-level jobs which involved in-stalling and testing phone circuits. My job was to install, operate, maintain and troubleshoot computers used by the technicians to test circuits and write trouble tickets. I enjoyed this; it was challenging and ever-changing as a blur of new computers were rolled in every couple of years as the indus-try progressed. But in the background there were already hints of a dark side emanating from AT&T's secretive top-level connections with the federal government and the De-fense Department.

The high-rise Thomas St. facility, built in 1974, was reput-edly designed for nuclear war and evoked a gloomy Kafka-esque world: There were no windows, as the outside was clad in giant pink granite slabs, while the internal structure had tons of reinforced concrete and, said the rumors,[2] spe-cial shielding against the electromagnetic pulse from high-altitude nuclear detonations that could fry unprotected electronics and electrical equipment. With its own emer-gency generator, a closed environment that could protect against nuclear fallout, and a well-equipped but unused cafeteria, it had the flavor of a '60s "fallout shelter."

Each floor had the unusual height of eighteen feet to ac-commodate the phone company's switching equipment, with fluorescent lighting in the work areas and stark concrete walls. Company efforts to save on electricity by turning out

---

2. There's more than just rumors. For instance, see the unclassified doc-ument, "Electromagnetic Pulse (EMP) Survivability of Telecommunica-tions Assets," Feb. 6, 1987, issued by the National Communications System in Washington. This highly technical analysis of the threat of high-altitude EMP to the AT&T system in nuclear war speaks of an "EMP mitigation program" initiated years earlier by presidential direc-tive, and warns that "building shielding integrity" may be compro-mised by "apertures" such as "windows."

some lighting in the hallways added to the gloom. The computer room where I was assigned to work was always cold from the blast of air conditioning to cool the computers, so one often needed a sweater. Without a view of the outside world, one could easily lose track of day and night, like duty in a missile silo.

When I first arrived, they were relying on DEC PDP-11 computers, which used Bell Labs' UNIX operating system. These were soon replaced by the DEC VAX-11/780, which became the workhorse for a few years. The computers had hundreds of half-inch-thick cables connected to them which ran under the raised floor to telecommunications equipment, which allowed technicians in distant offices to access the software remotely. We rotated tours (shifts), and when I was on the night tour we did the backups, using multiplatter disc drives the size of washing machines.

One day in the late '80s I had an inkling of the technological revolution coming. One of our computers, made by Western Electric (the traditional and now-defunct manufacturing arm of AT&T) was used for recordkeeping and had over a hundred cables connected to modems for remote access. A new technology was suddenly installed on an experimental basis: All the cables were removed and replaced by a single fiber-optic cable the thickness of a martini straw. At the same time, I heard that there were desktop-size disc drives with far more storage capacity than our washing-machine drives, and other miniaturized wonders were in the offing.

The handwriting was on the wall. It was becoming obvious that this large computer room could eventually be reduced to a much smaller space with far fewer workers. In 1989 they started the almost-yearly "downsizing" and never stopped. In the first wave I was forced out of the computer room because I was the last hired and hence was low on seniority, so people like me were henceforward perennially in jeopardy.

After that my work history at the company reflected the endless moving from city to city which many did to stay ahead of the ax-men and/or find some less stressful job. From the computer room in Manhattan I took a transfer to White Plains to save my job. But it was one of those cubicle jobs so accurately portrayed in Dilbert cartoons by Scott Adams, who had worked for a phone company.

The job was driven by computer assignments on your "zone," and you had to meet daily due dates with compulsory entries into the computer, combined with often-stressful phone calls with angry customers and sometimes hours-long testing of circuits long-distance on your computer screen. My chronic asthma was exacerbated and I had to go to the emergency room numerous times. Then I saw there were some openings in Pleasanton, California, so I grabbed the chance to go to the milder climate of the San Francisco Bay Area.

The return to California was a big relief, but still it was another cubicle situation. At one point I found a brief respite when I noticed an opening for a tech job at AT&T's marine radio station KMI, which provided telephone connections for ships at sea. It was located in the beautiful national park at Point Reyes and was a dream job. My FCC license enabled me to get it despite my low seniority. But after nine months, they started downsizing there too, and I was among the first to go, back to Pleasanton. (Eventually all three marine radio stations run by AT&T were closed down, replaced by satellite phones.)

Finally I found a way out when an opening arose in San Francisco to which I transferred in January 1998, and worked there for nearly six years. It was another computer room, located in leased space at 49 Geary St. in the city. It was originally known as EasyLink Services when it was acquired by AT&T a few years earlier from the wreckage of Western Union, which had pioneered electronic messaging services. There were only two union technicians left, but due to the dot-com boom they were expanding and brought in four more, including myself, who were classified as Computer Network Associates.

During my service there, the office provided WorldNet Internet service, international and domestic Voice-over-Internet (VoIP), and data transport service to the Far East. We provided 24/7 coverage with two technicians on each tour at first.

The site manager who hired me, Don Henry, held the title of Field Support Specialist (FSS), of which the company had only about a dozen in the country. The FSS people had technical training but were in a nonunion management title and were dispatched within their assigned regions in the U.S. to provide higher-level technical troubleshooting. Particularly relevant for this story, some of the FSS people had security clearances.

FSS guys usually had their own truck and were dispatched from their homes. Don was an exception since he also ran our office. Besides Don, our office also had two other FSS people who had once worked there as union techs and still used the office as a mail drop and sort of home base, but they rarely showed up. They were Ski and Rick.[3]

In 2002 a drama began to unfold in this office involving a secret and illegal government spying operation.

---

3. I am only providing Don's full name because he was the only FSS person to come forward in the media—on the PBS/*Frontline* episode, "Spying on the Home Front," May 15, 2007.

Chapter 2

Enter the NSA

I WAS SITTING AT MY WORK STATION in the summer of 2002 when a startling e-mail popped up: It said a representative of the National Security Agency (NSA) would be arriving on a specific date for some kind of business.

A creepy feeling ran up my spine that something very sinister and wrong was about the happen. I knew the NSA's charter involved electronic snooping on foreign communications and they should not be working in the domestic telecommunications system. I had been an anti-war protester back in the Vietnam days of the 1960s and '70s, and I recalled the scandal that broke in Congressional hearings in 1975-76 that revealed the NSA had been used to spy on domestic dissidents. Then-NSA Director General Lew Allen was grilled in public by the famous Church Committee and did a *mea culpa* about its Operation Minaret in which the agency assembled "watch lists" on American citizens.

Those events were embedded in my mind since I had read James Bamford's groundbreaking book about NSA spying, *The Puzzle Palace* (1982). Legal warrants for domestic eavesdropping in the phone system were the prerogative of the FBI, not the NSA. This was very fishy.

To this day I don't know why someone higher-up chose to mention the full name of the agency involved, but there it was in black and white.

Don Henry himself reiterated the message to us in person, saying that the NSA agent would be interviewing Ski

DONALD HENRY
FRONTLINE Fmr. AT&T manager

Courtesy of Frontline/WGBH Educational Foundation. Copyright © 2008. WGBH/Boston
Don Henry on *Frontline*, May 15, 2007

for a special job. Five years later, after the story had been widely reported in the media, Don came forward in an interview with Hedrick Smith on PBS/*Frontline* (May 15, 2007) and corroborated this part of the story, explaining that the visiting NSA agent

> was doing background check for a security clearance for one of our field engineers. He was going to be working at the Folsom Street office and they were building a secure facility there.

Amazingly, the rest of the media totally ignored this corroboration from a former AT&T manager.

We had to know the agent was coming because in such a small leased office (Geary St.) there was no security guard; we technicians were the ones to decide who gets entry through our locked doors.

In the event, I happened to be the one who answered the door the day he arrived. The NSA rep was a middle-aged guy dressed in a business suit and tie, average height and weight and apparently not in good physical shape. His pallid face had a permanent sour expression etched on it, as if he had an upset stomach, and he was unsmiling and unfriendly, speaking as little as possible. I directed him to Don and Ski.

Meanwhile, in late 2002 the scandal about Admiral John Poindexter's "Total Information Awareness" (TIA) program hit the headlines, raising worries about illegal government electronic snooping. I frequently had political conversations with Don, and this subject naturally came up in the course of our commiserating with each other about the Bush administration's rightwing policies. The *New York Times* described TIA as follows:

> As the director of the effort, Vice Adm. John M. Poindexter, has described the system in Pentagon documents and in speeches, it will provide intelligence analysts and law enforcement officials with instant access to information from Internet mail and calling records to credit card and banking transactions and travel documents, without a search warrant.[4]

Gradually I started to connect the TIA program with the curiously simultaneous appearance of the NSA at our office, and the more I learned about what they were installing, and where, the more I was convinced the two were connected.[5]

---

4. John Markoff, "Pentagon Plans a Computer System That Would Peek at Personal Data of Americans." From The New York Times, Nov. 9, 2002. Copyright © 2002, The New York Times, All rights reserved. Used by permission and protected by the Copyright Laws of the United States. The printing, copying, redistribution, or retransmission of the Material without express written permission is prohibited.
5. To mollify critics in Congress, the name was changed to "Terrorism Information Awareness," and Poindexter was removed. Although Congress made a show of cutting off funding in 2003, "elements" of the program survived in the deeper parts of the intelligence budget, including an obscure office on data mining called the Advanced Research and Development Activity or ARDA.

At first I thought I would never hear about the hush-hush job. It was obviously authorized at the highest levels and, since I did not have a security clearance, I would not be told the details anyway. The political atmosphere in the country after 9/11 had a witchhunt feel to it, and even modest criticism of the administration was getting painted as disloyalty or worse. I did not want to even appear to be probing into the secret project, and so I deleted the e-mail announcing the NSA visit—something I came to regret later.

But technicians talk. During the fall of 2002 word spread that a "secret room" was being built in the central office at 611 Folsom St., another virtually windowless phone building, not far from our Geary St. location. Near the end of the year we were assigned a new supervisor who was also in charge of two old-line AT&T central offices, one at Bush Street and the other at 611 Folsom Street, both located inside SBC buildings in San Francisco (a legacy of the breakup of the old Ma Bell).

Photo by Mark Klein
AT&T/SBC building at 611 Folsom St. in San Francisco

As part of getting acquainted, we went over to visit the Folsom Street office, and the techs gave us a tour of their domain. It was on this tour in January 2003 that we saw firsthand that the company

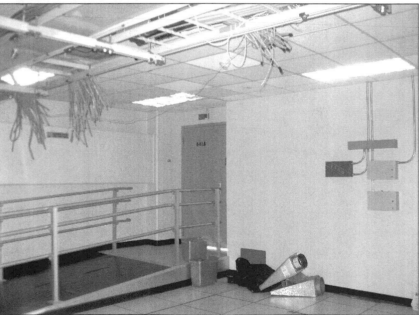

Entrances to secret room 641A in AT&T's central office at
611 Folsom St. in San Francisco

was building a secret room on the 6th floor to house some kind of equipment, and the union techs could not go in there—only Ski, who held a nonunion management title, was allowed to work in there. Right off, this angered the techs on contractual grounds, since Ski was working on the kinds of equipment that the union techs were supposed to handle, but they were barred from even entering the room.

So I deduced from the irregular and highly-restricted access rules, and Ski's involvement, that this was an NSA installation, and the first thing I worried about was the fact that it was on the 6th floor right next door to the 4ESS phone switch, the traditional workhorse used for AT&T long-distance phone calls. Now my mental alarm bells were ringing, but for the moment there was nothing to do but take some mental notes, particularly since it was not clear exactly what they were doing.

Meanwhile, the dark clouds of downsizing were gathering over the Geary St. office. Our office reported to the Network Operations Center (NOC) in Bridgeton, Missouri, and what happened there in early 2002 was an ominous sign of what was coming: The entire workforce of 116 Computer Network Associates (called CNA3) were suddenly fired and replaced by nonunion workers.[6] Over the next year the fired union workers were gradually hired back in a nonunion title.

I did not know it at the time, but it came out later that this union-busting was accompanied by the installation of an even more elaborate secret room in the Bridgeton NOC, the center of AT&T's WorldNet network. It had "the earmarks of a National Security Agency operation," Kim Zetter

---

6. Feb. 20, 2002 CWA report posted at
www.cwa-comtech.org/barg_mobe/page.jsp?itemID=27449261

reported in Salon.com,[7] including a sophisticated "mantrap" entrance using retina and fingerprint scanners.

This was right before the national contract was set to expire, but shockingly, the National union did nothing, and Local 6377 was left to mount a *pro forma* picket line for a few days, after which the Local actually disappeared from the CWA online directory for several years.

A few months later the New York CNA3s were eliminated, and by mid-2003 we heard they were planning to liquidate our entire Geary St. office in San Francisco. The scramble was on to find another job or be laid off.

Over the next few months our job gradually transformed into packing and shipping equipment, and trashing the obsolete hardware, as we prepared to close the office. A lot of the services and equipment, particularly the WorldNet Internet installation, were to be transferred to the Folsom St. office, so naturally we argued that we should go there with it.

But this required calling in the union to argue with the company, which preferred to throw us out with the old equipment. The jobs at Folsom St. were in the old title of Communications Technician, so we would have to be admitted back into that seniority list. In the end, the company relented and allowed three[8] of us to go to the Folsom St. office. My job was saved by a hair.

As we were literally closing shop in the fall we were visited by our *de facto* second-level manager, Morgan, who was based in Bridgeton. He took us to lunch to say goodbye. At one point in the conversation he mentioned this strange new construction of a room in Bridgeton. He said it was "creepy,"

---

7. Kim Zetter, "Is the NSA spying on U.S. Internet traffic?", Salon.com, June 21, 2006.
8. The company refused to admit the fourth CNA3, a Filipino-American woman with 25 years service, on the flimsy excuse that she had never been a Comm Tech, so she lost her job.

surrounded by secrecy and only certain people could enter, presumably not Morgan.[9] What really made it stick in my mind was that he said there was a logo on the door—the eye-over-the-pyramid icon which is on the back of dollar bills—and that got my attention because I knew that that was for awhile the logo of the Total Information Awareness program, until it became such a laughingstock that they withdrew it.[10]

A chill ran up my back: This thing was a lot bigger than I thought, and I was about to be transferred into the same office where I would be working practically on top of it.

---

9. Curiously, the following year Morgan was abruptly fired under murky and mysterious circumstances.

10. The eye-over-the-pyramid is often associated with various nutty conspiracy theorists, and it was sort of a fulfillment of paranoia that a government office would adopt that logo, but DARPA/TIA did so— you can still find it in the web archives.

Chapter 3

Vacuuming Up the Internet

WHEN AT&T WAS BROKEN UP in the divestiture process of the 1980s, the artificiality of the "separate companies" legal doctrine being propagated was demonstrated by what happened in the massive multistory central offices across the country. In reality, there was still one giant phone system across the county, and the local/regional companies (New York Tel, Pacific Tel, etc.) were by necessity physically interconnected with the long-distance AT&T in these offices which housed the phone switches. The "separate companies" theme's main use was to split up the union contract into numerous separate pieces and play the various workforces against each other.

The central office at 611 Folsom St. exemplified this situation. After divestiture AT&T's domain was reduced to the 6th, 7th and 8th floors where the long-distance equipment was concentrated, including the workhorse 4ESS phone switch. But a stroll through the office would reveal massive tree-thick size bundles of cables going up and down through the floors and ceiling, connecting these floors with the local company which controlled the rest of the building (Pacific Tel, later SBC). Troubleshooting problems often required collaboration between the AT&T technicians and the "other" companies' technicians.

These three floors might have once required scores of technicians to man them, but after decades of automation, there were only about a dozen covering all tours in two buildings. This meant typically there would be only four people assigned to the day tour, and considering their hours were individually different, and there were frequent absences due to vacation time, sick time, etc., one might often be working the whole office alone. (The supervisor was often not even there, since it had become possible for him or her to work from home using a laptop to monitor events and e-mail or phone the technicians.)

The job was driven by the electronic trouble-ticket system known as WMS (Work Management System, pronounced "Wee-Miss"). WMS tickets would stack up in your computer, prioritized by various levels of urgency, and the supervisor could easily track its progress from her home laptop. Servicing the ticket might be as simple as replacing a circuit pack at a particular location, or testing a long-distance circuit using your test set while on the phone with a technician in a remote office. Big disasters and outages would of course escalate up the management hierarchy and more help would be sent in.

We were responsible for trouble calls on all three floors, but for the sake of dividing up labor, each of us was assigned an area of primary responsibility—hopefully one that you were more familiar with. This meant the volume of trouble tickets you normally had to worry about was reduced, barring absences or other unforeseen events, and you could more efficiently deal with stuff about which you had more experience and knowledge. For instance, there were only certain technicians assigned to the 4ESS phone switch, since that required lengthy training that I did not have in my background. So partly because of my training, and partly out of a roll of the dice, the supervisor assigned me to the 7th floor Internet room, which turned out to be fateful.

The Internet room contained row after row of routers and related equipment, interconnected by thin yellow fiber-optic cables. The long-distance fiber circuits came into the building on the 8th floor, and then were distributed down to the 7th floor where they connected with the various routers, whose purpose was to route the data packets according to their addressing information.

Interconnecting one piece of equipment with another was accomplished with standard Lucent patch panels. Each panel contained 72 jacks for 36 circuits (two jacks for each circuit's Transmit and Receive functions). The rear jacks were semipermanently connected to the various pieces of equipment such as a router, so you only had to plug a pair of fiber cables into the frontside jacks to be connected to a particular router, and the other end of the fiber pair would be plugged into another panel depending on where the engineering called for it to go. Thus wiring up a new circuit, which was part of my job, involved the relatively simple task of connecting one panel's jacks to another panel using pairs of yellow fiber-optic cables. After that, of course, you had to test it to make sure it worked.

In the first days on my new job I walked around trying to familiarize myself with the office and particularly the 7th floor. Naturally I also tried to satisfy my curiosity about the "secret room" on the 6th floor, which had two doors labeled "641A." It was actually a room-within-a-room, the outer room containing long-established computer equipment for mundane corporate uses. While working in the outer room, you could walk around three sides of the secret room, which I measured to be about 24 by 48 feet. In the rear of the outer room there was a door which led you into the huge 4ESS switch room, which contained row after row of equipment and a tangle of cabling going up and across the ceiling.

The long-time technician in the Internet room, Bob, was assigned to train me. As it turned out, he decided to take the company's October buyout package, which was typically being offered every quarter to induce the older workers to retire. This meant there were only two months left for Bob to train me before he left the payroll, so I tried to make the most of it to learn about everything.

Every now and then Ski would pop into the office, sometimes stopping by to chat a bit with the techs, and then going to work in the secret room, which people jokingly called "Ski's room" or sometimes the "SIMS room," using a mysterious acronym that was referenced in one of the AT&T engineering documents, even though no one knew what SIMS stood for. I soon discovered that Bob and some of the other technicians had two of these documents, which they had to have in order to know what to do during the installation of the critical "splitter cabinet" back in early 2003.

One day as Bob was clearing off his desk for the last time, he handed me the documents and said, "You want these?" as he prepared to throw them out. I said sure, any knowledge could only be helpful in my new job. The documents were titled "SIMS Splitter Cut-In and Test Procedure Issue 2, 01/13/03," and "SIMS Splitter Cut-In and Test Procedure OSWF Training Issue 2 January 24, 2003." OSWF stands for On-Site Work Force, and these were obviously instructions to the technicians on how to "cut-in" or insert the "splitter cabinet" into working circuits in February 2003. There were 63 pages in all.

The documents showed where and how the mysterious splitter cabinet was to be cut-in to the already-working circuits, which required setting aside time in a late-night maintenance window to do the procedure. But what was its purpose? Perhaps the most revealing page was the last page of the second document, which listed 16 "Peering Links" that were to be cut into. These linked AT&T's network with other major carriers and Internet exchange points.[11] The 16 in the list were: ConXion, Verio, XO, Genuity, Qwest, PAIX (Palo Alto Internet Exchange), Allegiance, Abovenet, Global Crossing, C&W, UUNET, Level 3, Sprint, Telia, PSINet, and MAE West.[12] This page also revealed that the work was completed by the end of February 2003.

Naturally there was curiosity about what the secret project was doing. One day I was talking to Bob, who knew the office like the back of his hand, and I remarked, "It seems obvious to me, given that the secret room is next door to the 4ESS, that they're listening to phone calls." He shook his head and responded, "No, Internet."[13]

Indeed, I was not able to find any obvious physical connection between the phone switch and the secret room, but by tracing the cabling I could see the secret room was physically connected to the "splitter cabinet" in the 7th floor Internet room. One more document I came across confirmed this.

Every once in a while one of the FSS people would show up to work on various specialized equipment that only they were familiar with and was not inside the secret room. In order not to offend union requirements, they would typically ask for a union tech to help them. Thus one day in late 2003 Don Henry came in and asked me to help him in replacing some back-up batteries in one bay of equipment. By

---

11. Internet exchange points are facilities at which major Internet service providers interconnect their respective networks, thereby facilitating the flow of data packets around the world.

12. MAE stands for Metropolitan Area Exchange (or Ethernet).

13. One expert I talked to in 2007 pointed out that since AT&T was aggressively transferring its old long-distance phone traffic onto Internet fiber cables, it was therefore very likely that the splitter was picking up the traditional phone traffic as well as e-mail and other Web traffic.

coincidence, I had noticed a few days earlier that there was a thick AT&T engineering document (58 pages) lying in this area on top of a router, but I had left it alone in case someone might claim it.

As we were working, Don picked up the abandoned document and said, "I think this is Ski's, why don't you give it to him when you see him," and he handed it to me. I said sure. It was titled, "Study Group 3 LGX/Splitter Wiring San Francisco Issue 1, 12/10/02." LGX was a reference to the Lucent LightGuide patch panels.

Later I took the document back to my desk and went through it page by page, and soon I nearly fell out of my chair. This was a wiring document, sequential pages of tables with numbers and diagrams, showing precisely the connections between numerous panels and jacks. It documented that the splitter cabinet in the 7th floor Internet room was directly connected to panels in the 6th floor secret room, which was referred to as the "SG3 Secure Room." The other two documents made repeated references to the "Splitter," "Splitter Cabinet," or other descriptions which made it clear that the three documents were linked together.

Judging by the title, it's clear that SG3 stands for Study Group 3, an apparent attempt to make a sinister operation look innocent. And since San Francisco was number 3, it was evident that there were more such installations in other cities, a fact which was soon confirmed to me. I had a hand on only one small part of a giant octopus.

So what exactly were they doing? I looked for clues by going through the documents, and while closely examining the SG3 document, I suddenly had another "aha!" moment. In the equipment list on the "Cabinet Naming" page for the project, there was the usual hardware such as Juniper routers and Sun Servers and then, suddenly, something I'd never heard of before: a Narus STA 6400. What was that? I looked it up, and it turned out this was a very sophisticated and specialized product that not only was perfectly suited for sorting through the data stream in real time looking for things, but it was already being marketed specifically to telecommunications and other companies for intelligence and police spying.

I pulled it all together in a January 2004 memo[14] to which I appended eight pages from the AT&T engineering documents, two photos and some web pages which enhanced the Narus aspect.

The splitter was the first step in the spying operation. It simply made copies of the *entire data stream* and sent it to the secret room for further analysis, as I wrote in my memo:

> In order to snoop on these [Internet] circuits, a special cabinet was installed and cabled to the "secret room" on the 6th floor to monitor the information going through the circuits…. [The SG3] document addresses the special problem of trying to spy on fiber optic circuits. Unlike copper wire circuits which emit electromagnetic fields that can be tapped into without disturbing the circuits, fiber optic circuits do not "leak" their light signals.[15]
> In order to monitor such communications, one has to physically cut into the fiber [light signal] somehow and divert a portion of the light signal to see the information.
> This problem is solved with "splitters" which literally split off a percentage of the light signal so it can be examined. This is the purpose of the special

---

14. See Appendix A, "AT&T Deploys Government Spy Gear on World-Net Network," 16 Jan. 2004. The 8 pages of AT&T documents were later officially released by the company on June 12, 2007, after negotiations with the court in which AT&T was forced to admit that all the documents are genuine.
15. To be precise, we should admit that it is possible to force light to "leak" from the fiber by bending it too sharply, but this degrades the signal and is not the normal operational mode.

cabinet referred to above: circuits are connected into it, the light signal is split into two signals, one of which is diverted to the "secret room." The cabinet is totally unnecessary for the circuit to perform—in fact it introduces problems since the signal level is reduced by the splitter—*its only purpose is to enable a third party to examine the data flowing between sender and recipient on the Internet.*

The physical splitter itself typically consists of a special glass prism which splits the laser light beam emitted by the optical fiber into *two separate light signals:* One goes onward to its normal destination, the other is sent to the secret room. The important fact is that *each separate signal contains all the information,* nothing is lost, so in effect the entire data stream has been copied.[16] (This is analogous to a TV splitter at home which makes copies of the signal for two different rooms, except the TV splitter uses electrical signals instead of light signals and hence carries a lot less information.)

What screams out at you when examining this physical arrangement is that the NSA was vacuuming up *everything* flowing in the Internet stream: e-mail, web browsing, Voice-Over-Internet phone calls, pictures, streaming video, you name it. The splitter has no intelligence at all, it just makes a blind copy. There could not possibly be a legal warrant for this, since according to the 4th Amendment warrants have to be specific, "particularly describing the place to be searched, and the persons or things to be seized." It was also a blatant violation of the 1978 Foreign Intelligence Surveillance Act (FISA), which calls for specific warrants as required by the 4th Amendment.

---

16. A simple analogy can be made with using a flashlight at night to send a Morse code signal to someone. If you split off part of the light-beam with a mirror to send it to a second person, both would still see all the flashing information.

This was a massive blind copying of the communications of millions of people, foreign and domestic, randomly mixed together. From a legal standpoint, it does not matter what they claim to throw away later in their secret rooms, the violation has already occurred at the splitter.

Former NSA analyst Russell Tice came forward on January 21, 2009—deliberately the day after Bush left office—and confirmed to Keith Olbermann on MSNBC's *Countdown* that the NSA "had access to *all* Americans' communications, faxes, phone calls, and their computer communications," and used it to spy "24/7" on innocent domestic groups such as "U.S. news organizations and reporters and journalists."

My research on the Narus, documented in my 2004 memo, completed the basic picture of the spying operation:

> One of the devices in the "Cabinet Naming" list is particularly revealing as to the purpose of the "secret room": a Narus STA 6400. Narus is a 7-year-old company which, because of its particular niche, appeals not only to businessmen (it is backed by AT&T, JP Morgan and Intel, among others) but also to police, military and intelligence officials. Last November 13-14 [2003], for instance, Narus was the "Lead Sponsor" for a technical conference held in McLean, Virginia, titled "Intelligence Support Systems for Lawful Interception and Internet Surveillance." Police officials, FBI and DEA agents, and major telecommunications companies eager to cash in on the "war on terror" had gathered in the hometown of the CIA to discuss their special problems. Among the attendees were AT&T, BellSouth, MCI, Sprint and Verizon. Narus founder, Dr. Ori Cohen, gave a keynote speech. So what does the Narus STA 6400 do?
>
> "The [Narus] STA Platform consists of standalone traffic analyzers that collect network and customer usage information in real time directly from the message.... These analyzers sit on the message pipe into the ISP

[Internet Service Provider] cloud rather than tap into each router or ISP device" (*Telecommunications* magazine, April, 2000). A Narus press release (1 Dec., 1999) also boasts that its Semantic Traffic Analysis (STA) technology "captures comprehensive customer usage data...and transforms it into actionable information... [it] is the only technology that provides complete visibility for all Internet applications."

In other words, the Narus enables them to look at the *content* of every data packet going by,[17] not just the addressing information. It is the dream machine for a police state, one that even George Orwell could not imagine. Not only does it enable the government to see what millions of people are saying and doing every day, but it can build up a database which reveals the *connections among social groups— who's calling and e-mailing whom.*

Such a device can easily be turned against all dissident protest groups, and even the Democratic and Republican parties, with devastating effect. And it's in the hands of the executive power, in total secrecy.

It's evident from the revealed setup that the Narus provides the first level of sorting and selection, and it can be reprogrammed at any time to change the parameters for the search. The documents reveal that the secret room is equipped with its own private "backbone" circuit which obviously provides the path to forward whatever is collected to some remote, unknown location for further analysis and presumably permanent storage. Where would that be?

Curiously, William M. Arkin reported[18] in his column

---

17. Except perhaps for encrypted data, though the NSA's capabilities here are open to debate.
18. William M. Arkin, "NSA Expands, Centralizes Domestic Spying," *Washington Post,* Jan. 30, 2006

"Early Warning" in the *Washington Post* in early 2006 that the NSA was "building a new warning hub and data warehouse" in the Denver suburb of Aurora, and transferring personnel there from its historical center in Ft. Meade, Maryland. Arkin quoted from *Government Executive Magazine*, which boasted that the massive new data center "will be able to hold the electronic equivalent of the Library of Congress every two days." He concluded that the facility is the hub of data mining. Over months and years, the database would be huge, ready for data mining whenever the government wants to go after someone.

Another vast expansion of NSA data storage capacity has come in the San Antonio, Texas, region, as revealed by James Bamford in his book, *The Shadow Factory* (2008). Probably not by coincidence, the massive new NSA warehouse was quietly revealed only three months after Microsoft announced plans in January 2007 to put its new $550 million, 470,000-square-foot data center in the same area. "For an agency heavily involved in data harvesting, there were many advantages to having their miners next door to the mother lode of data centers," Bamford wrote. While the Microsoft center was automated and so needed only about 75 people to maintain the equipment, "the NSA was planning to employ about fifteen hundred" in an identically-sized data center, which suggests a massive data mining operation.

I realized I was wiring up the Big Brother Machine, and I was not happy about it—I had not signed up to be a spy for the NSA, but to maintain the public telecommunications system. But what could I do? It was apparent that the orders for this came from very high up, and it would be of no use to complain to the supervisor: She probably knew next to nothing about it and it was out of her hands anyway. And if I made a big stink, I would only become a target for a firing, or even some kind of government retaliation. So I decided to remain quiet and see what happened. As it turned out, there was more to discover.

I never got the chance to return the SG3 document to Ski, because in the fall of 2003 he was terminated as part of a downsizing which hit the FSS group. (Apparently there's no special reward for doing government work—the company's profit margins come first.) This prompted another visit by the NSA to the old Geary St. office before it finally closed; they wanted to meet Don there to discuss the qualifications of a replacement candidate, who turned out to be another FSS person, Rick.

One day I was wiring up a new circuit which the engineering required to go through the splitter cabinet. I connected the fiber pairs to the various panels and then called a provisioning tech in Atlanta so she could verify that the circuit worked. She could remotely access the appropriate router and send some test signals to verify the circuit, but it turned out it was not working properly—there were errors or even a complete loss of signal.

Suddenly, the provisioning tech remarked on the phone, "Gee, we're getting this same problem in the other offices where splitters are going in." I froze in my chair. "Other offices?" I asked. "Yeah, in Seattle and San Jose and San Diego and L.A.," she rattled off the cities as I jotted them down. In total astonishment, I repeated the cities to double-check what she had said. Later I also found that one of the documents specifically mentioned Atlanta as another site. This thing was getting bigger and bigger.

Meanwhile, I still had a problem to fix. I started tearing my hair out trying to figure out what was wrong, and finally I realized that these circuits used to work without the splitter, so let's see what would happen if I bypassed the splitter cabinet. Sure enough, when I did that the circuit came up normal and without errors. It dawned on me that the splitters added extra signal loss into the circuit, just enough loss that this particular router did not like it. The company was degrading the signal quality of its network for the sake of the NSA. But how could I fix this?

I called in Rick for help, since he was more familiar with the splitter cabinet. He arrived quickly, and after a moment's contemplation, he decided to get another splitter card for this circuit. The idea was to boost the signal level for my purposes by changing the split ratio: normally the splitter does a 50-50 split, but there were 60-40 and even 70-30 cards available. But to get a replacement he had to go downstairs and into the secret room where there was a storage cabinet of spares. He turned to me and said, "Want to come along?" I said sure.

I waited at the bottom of the rampway to Room 641A as Rick walked up and punched in the required code into the lock on the door—only he had the code—and he opened the door as I followed. To our right as we entered there was a desk against the wall, with a keyboard, mouse and screen sitting on it.

There were no great surprises, except to confirm that there was indeed a significant collection of hardware installed, humming away in rows of standard cabinets used by the telecommunications industry, plus a common industrial-size air conditioner (six feet high and somewhat wider). This was no small installation. Rick opened a storage locker and grabbed a spare splitter card. Before we left, he paused to open one of the equipment cabinets to show me the bundles of thick, yellow fiber-optic cables which had been incorrectly installed, causing problems for him: The tightly-bound bundles had overly sharp bends in them, a mistake which could cause data errors or even loss of signal.

On another occasion one day Rick literally stopped by the water cooler where some techs gathered, on his way to "Rick's room." There was the usual chitchat and somehow the conversation turned to Rick's job. He pulled from his shirt a bunch of keys hanging by a cord around his neck, and pointed to each one as he rattled off, "This one's for Seattle, this one's for San Diego..." and so on. It was a repeat of the list of cities I had already gathered on the phone, this time from the horse's mouth.

As 2004 ground on, I was increasingly disheartened by the situation I was stuck in. As it happened, the company put another buyout package on the table for people to grab, and since I was qualified, I decided now was a good time to go. So at the end of May 2004 I retired and started collecting my pension. But given the enormity of the crimes which I knew were being committed, it seemed prudent to keep the documents which were hard proof, in case there was some change in the political winds that would enable me to come forward and expose it. For the next year and a half this did not seem probable and I hid the documents away, figuring I would eventually throw them out.[19]

But the winds did change at the end of 2005.

---

19. At the end of 2004, Rick lost his job in yet another downsizing.

Chapter 4

The Story Breaks

LIKE A BOLT OUT OF THE BLUE, the *New York Times* broke the story in a December 2005 article which opened as follows:

Bush Lets U.S. Spy on Callers Without Courts

By JAMES RISEN and ERIC LICHTBLAU
Published: December 16, 2005

WASHINGTON, Dec. 15 – Months after the Sept. 11 attacks, President Bush secretly authorized the National Security Agency to eavesdrop on Americans and others inside the United States to search for evidence of terrorist activity without the court-approved warrants ordinarily required for domestic spying, according to government officials.

Under a presidential order signed in 2002, the intelligence agency has monitored the international telephone calls and international e-mail messages of hundreds, perhaps thousands, of people inside the United States without warrants over the past three years in an effort to track possible "dirty numbers" linked to Al Qaeda, the officials said. The agency, they said, still seeks warrants to monitor entirely domestic communications.

The previously undisclosed decision to permit some eavesdropping inside the country without court approval was a major shift in American intelligence-gathering practices, particularly for the National Security Agency, whose mission is to spy on communications abroad. As a result, some officials familiar with the continuing operation have questioned whether the surveillance has stretched, if not crossed, constitutional limits on legal searches.

"This is really a sea change," said a former senior official who specializes in national security law. "It's almost a mainstay of this country that the N.S.A. only does foreign searches."[20]

Risen and Lichtblau quickly followed up on this with a Dec. 24 article describing a vast domestic surveillance program: "Some officials describe the program as a large data-mining operation." I instantly knew this was connected to the sinister installation I had come across at AT&T and, sensing a shift in the political winds, I decided to try and bring it out into the light of day.

The administration immediately responded with a take-no-prisoners arrogance that was already its hallmark. Caught red-handed in illegal and unconstitutional activities, they would not apologize, they would not retreat, but instead launched an aggressive attack on all critics and mobilized the full power of the federal government to intimidate all opposition and justify their usurpation of power.

They went on a media campaign. Bush himself launched it in his weekly radio address on Dec. 17, 2005, the day after the initial *New York Times* article, saying the program was "to intercept the international communications of people with known links to Al Qaeda and related terrorist organizations...I have reauthorized this program more than 30 times since the September 11th attacks." The program soon was dubbed the "Terrorist Surveillance Program" (TSP) to sell it to the public.

---

20. James Risen and Eric Lichtblau, "Bush Lets U.S. Spy on Callers Without Courts." From The New York Times, Dec. 16, 2005.

Day after day, week after week, another leading member of the administration would openly argue for "the program" as a "necessary tool" in the so-called "war on terror." President Bush himself, Vice President Cheney, Director of National Intelligence John Negroponte, NSA Director General Michael Hayden, Attorney General Alberto Gonzales—all and more were trotted out to pound the media, which duly broadcast the propaganda without hardly a questioning comment.

At the same time, there was a calculated, reassuring and deliberately misleading subtext embedded in the message, that the so-called "terrorist surveillance program" was "limited" in scope, as Bush himself told reporters (*New York Times*, Jan. 2, 2006). And he outright lied, insisting the policy still was that "a wiretap requires a court order" and "nothing has changed":

> "When we're talking about chasing down terrorists, we're talking about getting a court order before we do so."

This *New York Times* report also claimed reassuringly that only "up to 500 phone numbers and e-mail addresses" were being eavesdropped on "at any one time." I knew this to be untrue, as the capabilities of the physical apparatus installed across the country would enable them to scan *billions of messages a second.*

They also talked mainly about phone calls while downplaying the Internet aspect, thus misleading people into thinking that if you don't call Al Qaeda in Afghanistan, you have nothing to worry about. "If you're talking to a member of Al Qaeda, we want to know why," Bush was often quoted saying.

Most people don't realize that their billions of Internet transactions, such as Web browsing, often go around the world on the Internet and thus could also be categorized as "international communications." Eric Lichtblau has revealed in his book *Bush's Law* (2008) that "despite the public focus on phone calls, most of the NSA's intercepts—75 percent by one estimate—were e-mails."

The administration's reassurances about the limited nature of the surveillance program apparently hung on lawyers' sophistry about the definition of "eavesdropping," arguing that vacuuming up the data by computer was not eavesdropping until they actually *looked* at it or *listened* to it. For instance, there was a hint at this distinction in a 2006 *Washington Post* story:[21]

> [NSA director] Hayden has described a "subtly softer trigger" for eavesdropping, based on a powerful "line of logic," but no Bush administration official has acknowledged explicitly that automated filters play a role in selecting American targets. But Sen. Arlen Specter (R-Pa.), who chairs the Judiciary Committee, referred in a recent letter to "mechanical surveillance" that is taking place before U.S. citizens and residents are "subject to human surveillance."…
>
> Even with 38,000 employees, the NSA is incapable of translating, transcribing and analyzing more than a fraction of the conversations it intercepts. For years, including in public testimony by Hayden, the agency has acknowledged use of automated equipment to analyze the contents and guide analysts to the most important ones.
>
> According to one knowledgeable source, the warrantless program also uses those methods. That is significant to the public debate because this kind of

21. Barton Gellman, Dafna Linzer and Carol D. Leonnig, "Surveillance Net Yields Few Suspects." From The Washington Post, Feb. 5, 2006.

filtering intrudes into content, and machines "listen" to more Americans than humans do. NSA rules since the late 1970s, when machine filtering was far less capable, have said *"acquisition" of content does not take place until a conversation is intercepted and processed "into an intelligible form intended for human inspection."* [My emphasis]

But in fact the illegal act happens *at the point of seizure* by the government, i.e., the splitter—not later, whether or not a machine is involved. That is the whole point of the 4th Amendment,[22] which demands the government get a warrant to show "probable cause" for seizing things, whatever the government does with it afterwards. What they do later is unknown, and at any rate, their word on anything has proven to be an exercise in prevarication.

Some experts, such as J. Scott Marcus, who submitted an expert analysis for the lawsuit against AT&T,[23] have pointed out that if the NSA wanted only international communications, then it would have been much more logical and economical to restrict the location of the splitters to entry points such as ocean cable-head stations, rather than put them in places like Atlanta and downtown San Francisco, where one would be sure to pick up massive volumes of supposedly unwanted domestic communications. As he described it in his declaration to the court:

> The majority of international IP [Internet Protocol] traffic enters the United States at a limited number of

---

22. The 4th Amendment reads: "The right of the people to be secure in their persons, houses, papers, and effects, against unreasonable searches and seizures, shall not be violated, and no Warrants shall issue, but upon probable cause, supported by Oath or affirmation, and particularly describing the place to be searched, and the persons or things to be seized."
23. "Declaration of J. Scott Marcus in Support of Plaintiffs' Motion for Preliminary Injunction," March 29, 2006

locations, many of them in the areas of northern Virginia, Silicon Valley, New York, and (for Latin America) south Florida. *This deployment, however, is neither modest nor limited,* and it apparently involves considerably more locations than would be required to catch the majority of international traffic. [Emphasis in original]

Marcus had held a top secret clearance when he worked as an FCC consultant on the Internet, and was personally familiar with AT&T's network from his own career experience. Commenting specifically on the AT&T documents I submitted, he wrote:

> "I conclude that the designers of the SG3 Configuration made no attempt, in terms of the location or position of the fiber split, to exclude data sources comprised primarily of domestic data.... Once the data has been diverted, there is nothing in the data that reliably and unambiguously distinguishes whether the source or destination is domestic or foreign."[24]

Though Marcus refrained from drawing the obvious conclusion, the facts strongly suggest that this entire apparatus was *designed for domestic spying.*

This point was highlighted by PBS/*Nova* in its program, "The Spy Factory," written and produced by James Bamford (Feb. 3, 2009). In one chapter, the show follows the huge data flow of Internet messages from Asia as it comes ashore in the U.S. at Morro Bay in southern California and thence to a small AT&T building in San Luis Obispo. "If you want to tap into international communications, it seems like the perfect place is San Luis Obispo," Bamford notes. "That's

---

24. This is because, unlike traditional wired home phone numbers which are unambiguously linked to street addresses, IP addresses are attached to equipment that could be located anywhere in the world, and pinning down their country of origin involves some guesswork.

where 80 percent of all communications from Asia enters the United States." But instead, the NSA tapped into the data stream hundreds of miles farther north—in the San Francisco AT&T office at 611 Folsom St., where they were certain to collect huge amounts of purely domestic traffic. This fact belies the government's claims that they're only looking at international communications

Furthering their attempt to minimize the program, administration officials endlessly repeated the mantra promoted by Bush himself: "One end of the communication must be outside the United States" in order to be monitored (*USA Today*, May 11, 2006). Again, from my knowledge of the physical apparatus, I knew this was not true, because the Internet data stream they were copying in San Francisco contained *all* communications, foreign and purely domestic, randomly mixed together. Even if you took them at their word, they would have to scan *all* of it in order to sort out the purely domestic from the supposedly international communications, and they could very well be storing the domestic communications for later analysis, while their lawyers argue it had not (yet) been eavesdropped on.

So it was no surprise to me when *New York Times* reporters Risen and Lichtblau revealed in 2009[25] that the NSA "went beyond" the legal limits of the latest FISA law in a "significant and systemic" way, and there has been an "over-collection" of Americans' *domestic* communications because of so-called "technical problems in the N.S.A.'s ability at times to distinguish between communications inside the United States and those overseas."

But the "improperly collected" domestic communications

25. Eric Lichtblau and James Risen, "N.S.A Intercepts Go Beyond Limits of Congress," April 16, 2009, and "E-Mail Surveillance Renews Concerns in Congress," June 17, 2009 in the *New York Times*.

are said to number "in the millions," and the NSA dragnet stores the vast e-mail collection in a database code-named "Pinwale," the *Times* revealed, used by analysts *since 2005!*

It's becoming evident this was not an accident: It was the *conscious purpose* of the original hardware design, and the FISA immunity bill passed by Congress in 2008 winked at the whole operation.

Then-Attorney General Alberto Gonzales tried to hide the broad scope of the TSP by a careful lawyer's parsing of words, such as in his testimony before the Senate Judiciary Committee in the summer of 2007,[26] repeatedly calling it the program publicly "described by the president" (about targeted phone calls), thereby trying to cover over *other still secret tentacles of the program*—particularly untargeted vacuum-cleaner data collection and data mining of the Internet. At the same time, he was using the heavy hand of the Department of Justice to silence any potential "leaks."

As early as December 31, 2005, the Justice Department announced that "it had opened a criminal investigation into the disclosure of classified information about a secret National Security Agency program" (*New York Times*). This was obviously intended to silence Congress, the media, and any potential whistleblowers inside the NSA who might have been tempted to come forward. The administration was manipulating the secrecy oath which people had taken to get security clearances, turning it into a weapon to silence anyone who had knowledge of wrongdoing.

This is when it dawned on me that I was "it," because I didn't have any security clearance and so was not bound by those rules and, by lucky happenstance, the documents I

---

26. "Gonzales to senators: 'I may have created confusion'," CNN.com, Aug. 1, 2007.

had were not classified. I was in a position to expose the operation without using any classified information.

But I still hesitated out of fear: Could I take on a giant corporation and the U.S. government, all by myself? Who would defend me? The political atmosphere still had a McCarthyite feel to it, in which any dissidents become the target of a lynch mob searching for "terrorists." But it occurred to me that the Risen/Lichtblau exposé of December 16 was a political indication of a shift at the top of government, a split of some kind which could provide an opening—perhaps on the order of the publication of the Pentagon Papers by the *New York Times* in 1971, which had signalled a desire to retreat from Vietnam. Maybe they would publish my material, I thought, and that would provide some protection.

So on December 31, 2005, I made my New Year's resolution: I would bring it all out into the public domain. I added a brief preface to my 2004 memo.

I carefully went through the 121 pages of AT&T documents and selected 8 pages which provided a good picture of the installation, and I appended them to my 2004 memo along with my two photos of the secret room, and my Web research on the Narus. Then I converted it to Acrobat PDF format. I also gathered some background material for reporters in another file, put it all on a CD, and made copies.

Not trusting the Internet for obvious reasons, I also anticipated using PGP (Pretty Good Privacy, a popular encryption program developed by Philip Zimmermann) whenever e-mail was necessary. I put my public PGP key on a floppy for whoever I was going to meet.

I was ready.

Chapter 5

Going Public
vs. Media Chickens

WITH MY INTRODUCTORY CD PACKAGE in hand, I started shopping online for people that would likely be interested. I remembered a couple of civil liberties groups whose websites were useful in the recent past, including the Electronic Privacy Information Center (EPIC), and the Electronic Frontier Foundation (EFF). Being a little nervous about using the phone for obvious reasons (I didn't think I was being spied on by the government at that point in time, but prominent civil liberties groups might very well be), I thought it best to just show up.

In early January I dropped by EPIC and gave them the CD along with a printout, and also a floppy with my public PGP key for secure communications. There was not much of any conversation: the lone lawyer in charge there took the package with a polite smile, and I left. A couple of weeks flew by.

Meanwhile, the administration was in the midst of their media campaign to justify the NSA spying program, and the daily lies were amplifying my frustration and anger. Why wasn't EPIC calling me back for more details? Time was wasting, while the media pounded the country with misleading propaganda.

So on January 20, 2006, a nice, sunny day, I took BART

into San Francisco and walked to the EFF office with my material. The receptionist sent me to see Shari Steele, Executive Director of EFF. After some minor questions about their work, I said something like, "I'm a retired AT&T technician and I have some information which would be of use to you."

Her eyes lit up. She went to get senior attorney Kevin Bankston, and we huddled in a back room as I presented my material. He was obviously extremely interested, and he called in a second senior attorney, Lee Tien, who rushed in very excitedly. They soon revealed that, unbeknownst to me, they were already preparing a lawsuit against AT&T regarding the illegal handing over of phone call records to the government. So of course I felt a sense of relief, that I had found the right place: a group that wanted to take on this fight.

An hour later as we wrapped up the meeting, I gave them my floppy with the PGP key on it, and they looked at me with disappointment. It turned out that they all have Macs, so they couldn't use the floppy. I burst out laughing at myself, thinking of that famous poem by Robert Burns about the best-laid plans of mice and men going oft awry— but this was a trivial problem solved by e-mail later.

Over the next few days, Kevin Bankston sent follow-up questions which I quickly answered, and by the end of the month EFF had filed its already-planned lawsuit against AT&T, which did not yet incorporate the information I had presented. Kevin e-mailed me, "I can't thank you enough for your brave willingness to speak out about this massive crime. We, and the rest of the country, owe you a great debt." This indeed was a group that was ready and eager to fight the government.

At this point in time my strategy was focused not on

lawsuits, but on publicizing what I knew, and on January 23 I started talking to an interested reporter for the *Los Angeles Times,* Joseph Menn, who was in the Bay Area and was covering the EFF lawsuit. Besides my prepared CD package, I gave him the full set of AT&T documents, the first time I had shown them to anyone. He seemed eager to do a big story on this, and over the next few weeks we had many exchanges by phone and e-mail as he worked diligently on what was promised to be a big front-page spread. It looked like this would finally hit the headlines.

Anticipating the blowback that would inevitably come, it suddenly became apparent that I would need a lawyer, which I did not yet have. After some referrals, I made contact with Miles Ehrlich and Ismail "Izzy" Ramsey in early February 2006. They were two young former assistant U.S. attorneys in San Francisco who had just resigned to start their own practice in a new Berkeley office. Indeed, when I first visited their office to get acquainted, there were still boxes stacked against the wall. They generously offered their services *pro bono* and have stood by me ever since, for which I am eternally grateful. We started training each other in our respective fields, with me describing the apparatus in the Internet spying operation, and them explaining the relevant aspects of the law. Our immediate task for the next few weeks was writing a statement for the public.

Another necessary path to follow was an approach to Congress, and it always helps to have some personal contacts. Kevin suggested I contact Senator Dianne Feinstein, and he gave me the phone number of her chief attorney in Washington, Steven Cash. I instinctively recoiled at the thought of trying to approach her as my memory of her record told me she was no friend of civil liberties, though she plays one on TV. My instinct was not wrong.

I called her attorney on the evening of February 1, 2006, and left a couple of messages on his phone. The next day shortly after 8 in the morning, I sent him a reminder e-mail, and he immediately called me. I quickly described what I had, and he expressed strong interest in seeing my material. After we verbally agreed on a PGP password for some minimal security,[27] I encrypted my usual package which included the sample pages from the AT&T documents and—according to my e-mail records—I sent it to him at 8:20 a.m.

The next day, a Friday, he called me at home, and I made notes of the conversation immediately afterwards:

> 2/3—1:50 pm—Steve Cash called, is very interested in the documents, wanted to verify that they are indeed tapping into fiber and copper circuits. Told him I can only verify fiber. He wanted to know if I knew specifically what they were doing in that room: I said I don't know, I don't have a security clearance, they might not be doing anything in that room, it's connected to the internet and the information it collects could go anywhere.
>
> He wanted to know if I know if they were indeed doing "unlawful interception," I said I don't have firsthand evidence of that, I don't have a security clearance. But I know only people with NSA clearance could go in that room and I know the president said they were doing wiretapping without a warrant, and that's unlawful in my eye.
>
> He said he would be in touch with me Monday.

But I never heard from him Monday, or ever again. And I was unable to get through to him or the senator. Later my well-connected attorneys ran into the same brick wall.

---

27. He did not have a public key to offer, so we had to use the simplest encryption.

The silent message was unmistakable: The senator did not want to sully her political skirts by having contact with a whistleblower. And this was a foretaste of her behavior and voting on this issue for the next two and a half years. At every turn, she was there pushing for immunity for the telecom companies in the Senate Intelligence and Judiciary Committees; peddling her toothless restatement of the "exclusive means" clause[28] of FISA as a substitute for any confrontation with the president over ongoing illegal NSA spying; ushering former NSA director Michael Hayden through his nomination for CIA director; and backing Michael Mukasey as a clone replacement for the resigning Attorney General Gonzales. Moreover, this ultimately turned out to be the attitude of virtually the entire Democratic Party leadership, not to mention the Republicans.

Meanwhile, in February 2006 I was anxiously waiting for that big story from the *Los Angeles Times*. Week after week went by, every so often the reporter called back to ask some more technical questions, tell me there was just a little more work to be done, and it would be out this Thursday, then next Monday, and so on. I was beginning to worry that they were getting cold feet. I was not wrong.

On Feb. 11 I got a call from Joe Menn, the *Los Angeles Times* reporter, who told me that their "top guy" was going to have a meeting with the Director of National Intelligence John Negroponte himself about this story over the weekend. I nearly fell down in shock—they were actually negotiating

---

28. The original Foreign Intelligence Surveillance Act (FISA) of 1978 stated that it was to be the "exclusive means" for doing legal domestic surveillance, so there was no need to restate it. The obligation of Congress was to *enforce* it on president Bush, who openly flouted the law. Feinstein's figleaf restatement of the clause was inserted in the final "retroactive immunity" bill passed into law in July, 2008, ironically making a mockery of the clause.

with the government on whether to publish! This merited a separate story itself, revealing the direct hand of the government in the editorial process of a major newspaper. More importantly, this meant that Negroponte knew about my documents—and me.

I now feared I was in great danger. Fortunately, I had anticipated precisely this turn of events, and so had already started communicating with the *New York Times* reporters two days earlier. Now I urgently felt they should know what was going on, so right after the call from Menn on the 11th, I sent an e-mail to James Risen that day:

> I just got a call from the LA Times reporter. He says "the forces of righteousness are not doing too well." Article was to go on Thursday 2-9, but then another LA Times reporter was going to talk to Feinstein's people, so they held off to see what she had to say. Feinstein's people said they thought my information is perhaps correct (that this is an illegal spy operation), and perhaps not—they rated it at 50-50.
>
> This estimate went up the food chain at LA Times. The top guys there estimate the probability of its correctness at 90%, but Joe says that while they are "honorable," they are suffering from being "chicken-hearted" and afraid of getting egg on their faces. Furthermore, on Friday (2-10) Negroponte exchanged messages with top guy of LA Times, and they will apparently talk over this weekend...And so [Menn] describes the chances for publication as "grim" and he is "demoralized."
>
> Then he went on to say that in seven years he has not seen a story "spiked" for "nefarious reasons," implying that this is exactly what is happening now.

My contact with the *New York Times* had begun on February 9, when I finally reached James Risen; he called in Eric Lichtblau as well ("It's important!" I could hear Risen saying to his colleague), and I started relating the story. They were very interested, and I sent them my abbreviated package of material. It was a good thing I got the ball rolling, because the *Los Angeles Times* story was already falling through, though it officially dragged on for weeks more.

I began to panic now because I was in the most vulnerable position: The government was on to me, but I did not yet have a published article and the protection that comes with publicity. I had visions, perhaps a bit paranoid in hindsight, of being disappeared in the night, like Karen Silkwood.

Menn's gloom suddenly turned to optimism on Feb. 13, as I e-mailed Risen and Lichtblau afterwards:

> The LA Times reporter called just now. He says he thinks he's "pulled the rabbit out of a hat." He says he's got verification of the story from a "high-ranking source" and is now working it into the story. He feels that now even the "top guy" at his paper will let it be published.

I felt badly for him: He was obviously an honest reporter who was diligently working on a great story, but the political forces against him were too immense. Finally on March 29 he told me that the story was officially killed, and he hadn't "emotionally recovered yet."

The following year I was working with *ABC Nightline* for my first national TV interview that was actually broadcast, and to their credit, they followed up on my story about the *Los Angeles Times*. In the accompanying online text report by Brian Ross and Vic Walter, they confirmed that the *Los Angeles Times* had been talking not only to Negroponte but also NSA director Hayden:

> The Los Angeles Times' decision was made by the paper's editor at the time, Dean Baquet, now the

Washington bureau chief of The New York Times.

Baquet confirmed to ABCNews.com he talked with Negroponte and Hayden but says "government pressure played no role in my decision not to run the story."

Baquet says he and managing editor Doug Frantz decided "we did not have a story, that we could not figure out what was going on" based on Klein's highly technical documents.[29]

Of course this was an absurd and flimsy excuse. They never heard of consulting experts? I think it's evident that they had capitulated to government pressure.

This was not the only instance of censorship. In the summer of 2006, after my story had already hit the news media, various national TV news shows approached us to get the rights to be "first out the gate" with an exclusive interview. We finally agreed to give it to *60 Minutes*, historically a well-known national icon of crusading TV journalism. In September they flew me to New York City, and on the 25th I was interviewed by Steve Kroft for a show produced by Janet Klein (no relation to me).

It was a good solid interview and they had a blockbuster news story. Then we waited, and waited, and waited, and they kept putting us off as to the air date. Four months flew by while my mouth was taped shut since we had given CBS an "exclusive," so I was silent during the entire 2006 election period. My lead attorney at this time, the well-known and well-connected Jim Brosnahan, was astonished: "This has never happened to me," he said, adding that they had "no good reason" on the phone for the delay. Finally in January

---

29. Brian Ross and Vic Walter, "Whistle-blower Had to Fight NSA, LA Times to Tell Story," March 6, 2007. The video and text can be found on Brian Ross' website at:
http://blogs.abcnews.com/theblotter/2007/03/whistleblower_h.html

2007 we gave up and accepted the offers from *ABC Nightline* and *Frontline*. It seems obvious to me that someone higher up at CBS had killed the story for political reasons, but could not tell us that, so they just put us off without explanation.

Throughout late February and March 2006 I was in a state of controlled panic. The *Los Angeles Times* story was falling through, and after an initial excited interest at the *New York Times*, they strangely stopped calling for weeks. Though Risen and Lichtblau were undoubtedly interested, I did not have the same confidence in their editors. Why didn't they call back? Were they sitting on the story just like they sat on their original NSA story for a full year?[30] Just to make sure they had the full picture, I e-mailed them the full set of actual AT&T documents in mid-February.

I wanted the information to get out to the public fast. I sent e-mail and snail mail to leading senators on key committees, but none responded. I sent my standard package to my own congressman, Pete Stark, who in the end was the only Congressperson who ever answered me directly. He wrote: "Thank you for sending me information about the NSA's spying program. I'll forward it to the Judiciary Committee so they can use it in their ongoing monitoring of the program." I never heard anything from the Judiciary Committee, or any other committee for that matter.

Meanwhile I was working on another path to breaking the story. On February 23 Kevin from EFF contacted me, asking if I would submit a legal declaration of what I knew.

---

30. When the *New York Times* published their original exposé about warrantless NSA spying on Dec. 16, 2005, they admitted that they had wavered after meeting with administration officials to discuss it, and had "delayed publication for a year." In August 2006 their executive editor, Bill Keller, also admitted that they had been sitting on the story even before the 2004 elections, thereby shielding the president from damaging pre-election news.

Five days later he asked for the full set of AT&T documents, which I sent him. I would now become a witness for the EFF lawsuit, *Hepting v. AT&T*.[31]

---

31. For the record, and contrary to common misconception, I was never a party to the lawsuit and thus had no financial stake in it if they had ever won any monetary judgments.

Chapter 6

Witness

THE FIRST ORDER OF BUSINESS in becoming a witness was to write a legal declaration which described what I knew. In collaboration with my lawyers we set about doing this, and went through several drafts over the weeks of March 2006. Finally at the end of the month it was ready.[32] But just as EFF was going to file it and the three AT&T documents at the courthouse, the federal government intervened.

The feds had gotten wind of the filing, and suddenly demanded to see the AT&T documents beforehand. The EFF had asked the court to file the material under regular court seal with the presiding judge, Vaughn Walker, but this was not good enough for the U.S. government: They expressed fear that there might be some classified information contained therein, and were threatening to put it in a "sensitive compartmented information facility," which would mean it could not be kept at the courthouse but only be in the possession of the federal government at a special highly protected secure location.

This would have made the whole legal process more difficult for everyone including the judge. But the upside was that the move got the attention of the media, which suddenly realized that my documents might be the real scoop. We started getting flooded with calls from reporters, including

---

32. See Appendix B, "Declaration of Mark Klein in Support of Plaintiffs' Motion for Preliminary Injunction"

the long-silent *New York Times*. The media logjam was broken.

For four days the feds held the documents, considering the matter. Then finally on April 4, 2006, they returned them to the EFF with a letter from Anthony J. Coppolino, Special Litigation Counsel for the Federal Programs Branch, which said: "The Department of Justice does not object to your filing under seal…the three documents you provided to us on Friday, March 31, 2006." This was legally significant: By agreeing to allow the documents to be filed under ordinary court seal, the feds admitted by implication that they did not contain any classified information. This would undermine their subsequent claim that "state secrets" were involved.

On April 6 we gave out our first press release, which recounted my discovery of the secret room and for the first time, revealed the pernicious role of the Narus equipment. This caused a sensation, particularly among the technical community of computer and software professionals, who immediately understood the implications. As I summarized it in my press release:

> Based on my understanding of the connections and equipment at issue, it appears the NSA is capable of conducting what amounts to vacuum-cleaner surveillance of all the data crossing the Internet—whether that be peoples' e-mail, web surfing, or any other data.
>
> Given the public debate about the constitutionality of the Bush administration's spying on U.S. citizens without obtaining a FISA warrant, I think it is critical that this information be brought out into the open, and that the American people be told the truth about the extent of the administration's warrantless surveillance practices, particularly as it relates to the Internet.
>
> Despite what we are hearing, and considering the public track record of this administration, I simply do not believe their claims that the NSA's spying program is really limited to foreign communications or is

otherwise consistent with the NSA's charter or with FISA. And unlike the controversy over targeted wiretaps of individuals' phone calls, this potential spying appears to be applied wholesale to all sorts of Internet communications of countless citizens.

The cat was out of the bag at last. And the government made no moves against me. However, AT&T now came after me.

The very same day as the press release, Miles and Izzy received a letter from AT&T making a series of demands. They claimed that I had wrongfully disclosed "confidential and proprietary information" which was "extremely sensitive in nature and could be used to compromise the integrity of AT&T's network." They made five lengthy demands, including the immediate return of "the originals and all copies" of the documents, and also outrageously demanded that I "refrain from discussing or otherwise disclosing your sealed declaration." They instructed my lawyers to respond by the next day. In response, we set up a meeting with AT&T attorneys the following Monday.

Miles and Izzy were experienced in criminal law, but AT&T's action would involve civil law, so they scrambled around for an experienced attorney in that branch of law, and we lucked out: James Brosnahan, senior attorney at the heavyweight firm of Morrison & Foerster in San Francisco, agreed to help. Brosnahan had decades of trial experience, had once been president of the San Francisco Bar Association, and knew how to deal with highly controversial cases (e.g., he had been the lawyer for John Walker Lindh). He agreed to come to the Ehrlich/Ramsey office in Berkeley on Saturday so we could all prepare for the Monday confrontation with AT&T.

AT&T had also sent a threatening letter to EFF, making similar false claims and demands. I felt EFF should have my technical arguments as to why the letter was false to the core, so I sent the following:

> Their letter is intended to dazzle ignorant people who know nothing about technical matters. Indeed, it is filled with either feigned ignorance or actual ignorance as to what the documents actually show.
>
> First they claim that the documents "relate to the technical structure of AT&T *telephone* networks" (my emphasis). Anyone with any technical knowledge can see that this is false. The documents show the connections to AT&T's *internet* service, not their telephone service. The "engineers" they consulted are either ignorant or deliberately misleading.
>
> Then they claim ominously that if the documents fall "into the wrong hands" they could "be used to 'hack' into the AT&T network, compromising its integrity." In fact, hackers require *IP addresses* to do their hacking. *There are no IP addresses in these documents.*
>
> As for the "integrity" of their network, it was working fine before they added their secret equipment. In fact, *they broke into it* in order to make copies of the data for some secret purpose, and that's what the documents demonstrate. Again, anyone with some technical knowledge can see that all this equipment has only one purpose: to make copies of the data and then sift through the data. They can argue over the purpose, but they cannot deny what the documents show.
>
> It is interesting to note that they do not categorically deny that these documents reveal a government spying operation; they merely state evasively that "it is *not clear to us at this point* whether these documents have any relevance to claims made in your clients' complaint" (my emphasis). Obviously they are hoping that all we have are documents and no witnesses. As for the government, they have taken the smarter tack and are letting AT&T provide cover for them in the guise of protecting "trade secrets."

As for the "trade secrets" angle, the fact was that the documents in and of themselves were common garden variety engineering showing the connections between standard Cisco routers, Lucent patch panels and other such well-known equipment. No trade secrets revealed there. AT&T was just covering for the government.

On Saturday I met with all the attorneys—including Brosnahan and his colleague Tony West, plus my original attorneys, Miles Ehrlich and Ismail Ramsey—and we spent the whole day going over my information and documents, and every other detail which might be relevant, such as my work history (e.g., I had numerous outstanding reviews from many supervisors over the years, a fact which could help refute any false charges of being a "disgruntled" worker). As Brosnahan realized the enormity of the issues at stake, including the fact that Senator Feinstein had already been sent some of the documents, he commented, "This is heavy."

One of the other lawyers joked that it sounded like a Hollywood script, and asked who would I like to play me in the movie version? I burst out laughing in this moment of comic relief, and then someone tossed out "Robert De Niro," to which I countered with Tom Hanks to complete the joke.

Getting back to seriousness, Brosnahan warned me of the possible consequences if AT&T decided to sue me and we lost—the worst case being the loss of my house and financial assets. In short, there was only danger in this effort,[33] but I was determined to press on and said I would not return the documents. At the end of the meeting Brosnahan came up to me and said, in a hint of the fighting Irish, "My grandfather

---

33. In fact, a week later Brosnahan arranged a meeting at his office so my testimony could be videotaped and stored in a safe, in case something untoward should happen to me.

would be proud of me for taking this on," and assured me, "Don't worry, Mark, we won't let you hang out there to dry." He was as good as his word.

It was not necessary for me to go to the Monday meeting; Brosnahan would represent me there. I wish I could have seen the faces on the AT&T lawyers when Brosnahan walked in on Monday. It was like a "John Wayne movie," he said later, with the hero facing down the villains and each side getting ready to draw, with the bad guys getting nervous and eventually standing down. Brosnahan told me he berated them at one point, "They made you work on an invasion of privacy!," putting them on the defensive. In the end they came to a sort of unwritten truce. In fact, the company was obviously forced to retreat because if they sued me we would get the right of discovery in court, and that was the last thing they wanted. They only wanted to get out of court.

After this meeting, they never came after me again or filed any suits, and they hid from the media with the endlessly-repeated mantra, "AT&T does not comment on matters of national security."

On April 7 the *New York Times* published their first mention of my connection to the lawsuit, but it was a puzzling three-paragraph note buried in the inside pages with no byline ("Court Filings Tell of Internet Spying"), saying that a "former AT&T technician" said the company helped the NSA in 2003 "to install equipment capable of 'vacuum-cleaner surveillance' of e-mail messages and other Internet traffic," and alluding to the secret room in San Francisco. Their only purpose seemed to be to signal the government that I had "provided" the *New York Times* with the documents, while minimizing the story for everyone else. It looked like some kind of backroom brawl was going on, but the public could not know the details.

70   Finally on April 13 they published a real article, "Docu-

ments Show Link Between AT&T and Agency in Eavesdropping Case" by John Markoff and Scott Shane. They had shown the documents to four independent technical experts.

The upshot: All four experts concluded that "AT&T had an agreement with the federal government to systematically gather information flowing on the Internet through the company's network." This was followed by an April 17 editorial titled, "AT&T and Domestic Spying." Finally it was out there in a major newspaper, though I noticed that the *New York Times* did not show any images of the actual documents, and never called me back for an in-depth followup story.

These experts' conclusions in the *New York Times* paralleled those of J. Scott Marcus, who had submitted a technically detailed 34-page analysis to the court for the EFF complaint in late March. His experience was at a much higher technical level than mine, and he had held a top secret security clearance when he was a member of the FCC's Homeland Security Policy Council, so I breathed a sigh of relief that my claims were not challenged but in fact were being verified and given much more credibility in his analysis:

> I conclude that AT&T has constructed an extensive— and expensive—collection of infrastructure that collectively has all the capability necessary to conduct large scale covert gathering of IP-based communications information, *not only for communications to overseas locations, but for purely domestic communications as well....*
>
> I am persuaded that the SG3 Configurations were deployed primarily in order to perform surveillance on a massive scale, and not for any other purpose.

Marcus estimated there were "15 to 20 sites" across the country, and extrapolating from his knowledge of AT&T's network, calculated that *"a substantial fraction, probably well over half, of AT&T's purely domestic traffic was diverted."* [All emphasis in original]

71

It was becoming clear that the government could not hide behind AT&T's claims of nonexistent "trade secrets" to keep the case from exposing the NSA. So on April 28 they announced they would invoke the "nuclear option"—the so-called "state secrets" doctrine—and intervene directly in the case to quash the lawsuit. But ironically this action only brought more news media attention, as it only confirmed in everyone's mind that this was indeed an NSA spying project, not some mundane company "trade secret." Why else would the government get involved?

The "state secrets" doctrine had become fully established in law at the height of the McCarthyite witchhunt in the early 1950s, so it was in a way a natural weapon for the Bush administration in the terror scare of the 2000s. In the 1953 case, *United States v. Reynolds,* relatives of civilian crew members killed in the crash of a military plane demanded the crash reports, but by invocation of the "state secrets privilege," they were denied on the grounds that the reports allegedly contained secrets about the military mission. In a revealing footnote, almost 50 years later the documents were released and it came out that there were no such secrets, only revelations about Air Force negligence in maintenance of the aircraft.[34] But the privilege became established as a "nuclear option," a way for the government to dismiss a lawsuit out of hand without the judge even examining the evidence.

So on May 13, the U.S. government made a Saturday filing for Judge Vaughn Walker, who was to preside over *Hepting v. AT&T,* in the U.S. District Court in San Francisco. Walker had been appointed to the bench by former president George H.W. Bush, but although he was a conservative, he

---

34. See SECRECY NEWS from Federation of American Scientists Project on Government Secrecy, Vol. 2004, Issue No. 8, Jan. 26, 2004

was known to be independent-minded with a strong libertarian bent. The government soon found he would not be a pushover.

Invoking "state secrets," the feds moved to dismiss the lawsuit and submitted sealed secret documents and a heavily edited public version, along with declarations from the Director of National Intelligence, John Negroponte, and the director of the National Security Agency, Lt. Gen. Keith Alexander. This was a big-stakes battle looming, and the government must have figured they were sure to win immediate dismissal.

The first hearing in the case was the following Wednesday, May 17, and the court in San Francisco was packed with people spilling out into the hallway. Brosnahan had rented a van to take me and all four of my attorneys, plus his communications manager Kerry Efigenio (who I very much appreciated for fielding the flood of media inquiries in those weeks, thereby protecting me from being inundated.)

We stepped out a block away from the courthouse and as we approached the building we were mobbed by reporters with notepads and TV cameras and microphones. Now I knew what it was like to be a public figure. They all wanted comments but I could not say anything until after the hearing. One woman discreetly slipped a piece of paper into my hand with her name and the phone number for *60 Minutes*. Once inside the courtroom, Tony West whispered in my ear that someone was wondering why Mark Klein needed so many lawyers, and I told him the answer should be, "How many lawyers has the government got?"[35]

---

35. Ironically, a few days after the Obama administration took over in Jan. 2009, Tony West was nominated to be an assistant attorney general in charge of the Justice Department's Civil Division.

Photos by Quinn Norton. Reprinted by permission

May 17, 2006, Mark Klein and his lawyers speak with the media outside the San Francisco courthouse: Above with James Brosnahan and Miles Ehrlich (rear). Below: flanked by Ismail Ramsey (left) and Tony West.

As soon as we entered, I found out that the AT&T lawyers were furious at me because of what had been posted at 2 a.m. that morning on the website of Wired.com.

Somehow Wired.com had gotten hold of my 2004 memo about the secret room, including the eight pages of AT&T documents and two photos of the secret room, all of which they posted online ("AT&T Whistleblower's Evidence," May 17, 2006). A week later Wired.com's Editor-in-Chief Evan Hansen explained their motivation in more detail. Though they confused my 2004 memo with my court-sealed legal declaration, it was true that all of the AT&T documents were still under court seal, as Hansen explained:

> A file detailing aspects of AT&T's alleged participation in the National Security Agency's warrantless domestic wiretap operation is sitting in a San Francisco courthouse. But the public cannot see it because, at AT&T's insistence, it remains under seal in court records.
>
> The judge in the case has so far denied requests from the Electronic Frontier Foundation, or EFF, and several news organizations to unseal the documents and make them public.
>
> AT&T claims information in the file is proprietary and that it would suffer severe harm if it were released.
>
> Based on what we've seen, Wired News disagrees. In addition, we believe the public's right to know the full facts in this case outweighs AT&T's claims to secrecy.
>
> Before publishing these documents we showed them to independent security experts, who agreed they pose no significant danger to AT&T. For example, they do not reveal information that hackers might use to easily attack the company's systems.[36]

---

36. Evan Hansen, "Why We Published the AT&T Docs," May 22, 2006. Copyright © 2006 Condé Nast Publications. All rights reserved. Originally published in Wired.com. Reprinted by permission.

To this day I don't know how they got it, but it wasn't from me, though I could not say I was unhappy about it. For the first time, the public could look at some of the actual documents and read my technical analysis of what they meant. Wired.com had more guts than the *Los Angeles Times* and *New York Times* put together. This was true courageous journalism.

The hearing was largely taken up with various preliminary maneuvers, and the first one was AT&T's attempt to muzzle me and get the court to order EFF and me to return all the documents and bar further disclosure. One of AT&T's many lawyers, David Anderson, whined that it "was just eight hours ago when Klein's statement in greater factual detail than ever before was placed out on the worldwide web." He demanded the return of the documents and a list of all people who had received them, and there was this exchange with Judge Walker, causing titters in the courtroom:

> THE COURT: Well, now, I can issue orders that bind the plaintiffs and bind their counsel, but Mr. Klein's not a party to this litigation, and Mr. Klein apparently has possession of these documents. So what I do with respect to plaintiffs and plaintiffs' counsel might very well be futile.
>
> MR. ANDERSON: Your Honor, we are here on the motion we've brought against these plaintiffs. As your Honor knows from the proposed order that we submitted and the briefing we submitted in support of it, we believe that the Court has the authority also to bind the plaintiffs' declarant [Klein], just as your Honor would have the authority to control the conduct—
>
> THE COURT: Is that part of my inherent authority again, Mr. Anderson? Oh, I'm liking this all the more.[37]

37. Official court transcript, United States District Court, Northern District of California, May 17, 2006

Since I was not a plaintiff in the lawsuit, the judge rightly figured he could not silence me, saying that "despite the rather encouraging view of federal judicial authority expounded by Mr. Anderson, I'm inclined to think the Court's authority is not quite that expansive." So he denied the motion, pointing out that AT&T was free to sue me if they wanted legal "remedies" on that score. My First Amendment rights still stood. This was a good judge.

As for the government's "state secrets" motion to dismiss, EFF attorney Cindy Cohn noted forcefully that

> It's plaintiffs position first and foremost that this can be litigated without reference to any state secrets; that the burden of proof under the statutes that we have claimed, that we have raised here is very straightforward. The question is whether the information has been acquired by AT&T in order to give it to the government and whether it's been divulged to the government and what the government does with that information afterwards, which I think could implicate state secrets, is completely irrelevant, or not necessary, for us to pursue this case.

With the government's motion filed, the case could not proceed until the judge decided whether to uphold the "state secrets" privilege. Another hearing was scheduled for June 23, and on that day the government made a very important admission about my evidence that undermined their motion for dismissal. The exchange went as follows, with the government's Assistant Attorney General, Peter Keisler, talking to Judge Walker:

> MR. KEISLER: None of the documents they [EFF] have submitted to accompany these declarations implicate any privileged matters.
>
> THE COURT: Including the Klein documents.

MR. KEISLER: We have not asserted any privilege over the information that is in the Klein and Marcus declarations.

THE COURT: Either in the declaration or its exhibits?

MR. KEISLER: We have not asserted a privilege over either of those. Mr. Klein and Marcus never had access to any of the relevant classified information here, and with all respect to them, through no fault or failure of their own, they don't know anything.[38]

While attempting to dismiss my evidence, Keisler had thus admitted that none of it was classified, so this meant the "state secrets" privilege did not apply to it or me. The implication was that there was no reason that the trial could not proceed in the open. The government had shot itself in the foot, and they were in for a shock.

On July 20 Judge Walker issued his 72-page decision. He ridiculed the government arguments and denied their "state secrets" motion. "AT&T and the government have for all practical purposes already disclosed that AT&T assists the government in monitoring communication content," he noted. "[T]he government has publicly admitted the existence of a 'terrorist surveillance program'.... Considering the ubiquity of AT&T telecommunications services, it is unclear whether this program could even exist without AT&T's acquiescence and cooperation."

The judge's thinking may have been assisted by our *amicus curiae* brief which we had submitted to the court in May.[39] It documented the huge quantity of detailed news media accounts of the so-called "terrorist surveillance program" and the associated technology that had already come to light.

---

38. Official court transcript, United States District Court, Northern District of California, June 23, 2006
39. See Appendix C.

"Mr. Klein's declaration and the information it relates regards information about publicly-known and publicly-discussed technology," we insisted.

Thus the administration's media campaign had backfired. "The very subject matter of this action is hardly a secret" anymore, Judge Walker argued in his July 20 decision, and the case should proceed: "[D]ismissing this case at the outset would sacrifice liberty for no apparent enhancement of security."

Going into panic mode, the government obtained a stay while they appealed to the Ninth Circuit Court of Appeals.

It took a year for the first and only hearing to take place. The case could not go forward during this time, reminding me of the old adage, "Justice delayed is justice denied."

The hearing room at the Ninth Circuit court in San Francisco was packed on August 15, 2007, and the overflow crowd (including me) was directed to another room where a closed-circuit TV was set up. It was clear from the testy exchanges that the three judges were not sympathetic to the government's ridiculous arguments. (Quotations are from Wired.com's coverage that day, cited below.)

Playing their only card—scare tactics—the government attorney, Deputy Solicitor General Gregory Garre, insisted that "Litigating this action could result in exceptionally grave harm to national security in the United States." Judge Harry Pregerson suggested that the court was being asked to "rubber stamp" the government's claim without knowing the facts, and challenged the government attorney, as reported in Wired.com/Threat Level:[40]

---

40. Kevin Poulsen, "NSA Judge: 'I feel like I'm in Alice in Wonderland',"with live blogging from the courthouse by Ryan Singel and David Kravets, Wired.com, Aug. 15, 2007. Copyright © 2007 Condé Nast Publications. All rights reserved. Originally published in Wired.com. Reprinted by permission.

"Who decides whether something is a state secret or not? ...We have to take the word of the members of the executive branch that something is a state secret?"

Garre counters that the courts should give "utmost deference" to the Bush administration.

Judge Pregerson: "What does utmost deference mean? Bow to it?"

Attorney Robert Fram presented the case for the EFF. He argued forcefully that their case can be made without using any classified information, just using the nonclassified "Klein documents":

"There is a splitter cabinet on the 7th floor on 611 Folsom Street. He (Klein) knows, because it was his job to oversee the room. He installed the circuits." Fram adds that "the splitter cabinet sends the light signal on the seventh floor [to] where the SG-3 study room is located."

Fram argues that the Foreign Intelligence Surveillance Act (FISA) allows people to challenge even the most secret electronic spying, by permitting courts to hear the government's evidence in chambers.

He's also carefully trying to say that EFF doesn't want any more information on sources and methods of the NSA, arguing that the mere existence of the secret room is good enough under the law to prove the existence of surveillance, regardless of what the government does once it has the internet packets.

"We have completed the privacy violation on the handover of the internet traffic at the splitter into the secret room, which room has limited access to NSA-cleared employees," Fram says. "What is not part of our claim is what happens inside that room."[41]

In the same hearing, the three judges also heard from the attorneys in the separate but related *Al-Haramain* case. In

---

41. Poulsen, Singel and Kravets, *ibid.*, Wired.com, Aug. 15, 2007

that case a now-defunct Islamic charity had accidentally been given a secret document by the government which revealed that they had indeed been illegally eavesdropped on, but the government immediately demanded its return and even absurdly tried to prevent the attorneys from using their *memories* of the document. Judge Michael Hawkins was incredulous and asked if it was really that secret:

> "Every ampersand, every comma is Top Secret?,"
> Hawkins asks.
> "This document is totally non-redactable and non-segregable and cannot even be meaningfully described," [Assistant U.S. Attorney General Thomas] Bondy answers.[42]

Eventually an exasperated Judge Margaret McKeown said, "I feel like I'm in *Alice and Wonderland.*"

It was clear to everyone that this panel would, if they ever issued a ruling, deny the "state secrets" claim and give the green light for the EFF lawsuit to go forward.

For the next year the administration scrambled to find another way to crush the lawsuit: an act of Congress.

---

42. Poulsen, Singel and Kravets, *ibid.,* Wired.com, Aug. 15, 2007

Chapter 7

"Updating" and Backdating FISA

THE WARRANTLESS "Terrorist Surveillance Program," as the administration dubbed it in accordance with their endless scare-mongering campaign, was a blatant violation of the FISA law, and everyone knew it. Indeed, it could have been grounds for impeachment. The FISA law itself had originated out of Congressional hearings in the 1970s after Nixon was caught trying to bug the Democratic Party National Committee headquarters at the Watergate hotel complex in 1972. Nixon was forced to ignominiously resign just as he was on the brink of being convicted by Congress.

The 1978 FISA law was passed supposedly to rein in such abuse of executive power. Though the secret court it created almost never went against the government, the Bush/Cheney White House would not tolerate even this modicum of oversight, and they ignored it.

But laws are of no use if they are not enforced. To do so now, Congress would have to confront the president himself: It would have been another Constitutional crisis that could only be resolved by impeaching the president and likely his cohorts such as vice president Dick Cheney and other key players. In 2006 the president was protected because his own party controlled Congress and functioned as a monolith in blocking any action against him. The widespread expectation was that the ostensible "opposition" party, the Democratic Party which had engineered the FISA law, would move to enforce it after they gained control of Congress in the November 2006 elections.

But my early experience with the Democrats in Congress, notably their refusal to even talk to me, made it clear, at least to me, that they had no stomach for such a fight, and some key leaders were in fact complicit in the crime. Indeed, throughout 2006 the only attempt to rein in the president came from a few liberal stalwarts such as Senator Russ Feingold, who in March 2006 submitted a bill to merely censure the president for illegal spying. But his own party leadership did not want even this slap on the wrist, and the measure died.

The administration's response to their exposure in 2006 was to start agitating for an "update" to the FISA law, which they argued was "30 years old" and not in tune with "modern technology" such as the Internet. This was disingenuous. Within weeks of the 9/11 tragedy, in October 2001 the administration rammed through Congress the omnibus "Patriot Act" which included specific updates for FISA, including giving the government expanded access to data from Internet service providers such as AT&T. It was a massive bill, so massive that many observed it could not have been prepared on such short notice and must have been on the agenda of the administration for a long time, awaiting some political opportunity.

Indeed, evidence has emerged that the NSA's illegal spying operation might have actually started before 9/11, as suggested in court papers filed by former Qwest CEO Joseph Nacchio. He "has alleged that the government withdrew opportunities for contracts worth hundreds of millions of dollars after Qwest refused to participate in an unidentified National Security Agency program that the company thought might be illegal,"as the *Washington Post* reported:

> Nacchio…said the NSA approached Qwest more than six months before the Sept. 11, 2001, attacks, according to court documents unsealed in Denver this week.
>
> Nacchio's account, which places the NSA proposal at a meeting on Feb. 27, 2001, suggests that the Bush administration was seeking to enlist telecommunications firms in programs without court oversight before the terrorist attacks on New York and the Pentagon. The Sept. 11 attacks have been cited by the government as the main impetus for its warrantless surveillance efforts.[43]

Qwest had also reportedly refused to hand over phone-call records of millions of Americans to the government, according to *USA Today*.[44] Nacchio's admirable reasons for refusal were described by his attorney, who exposed the illegality of the government's demands:

> "Mr. Nacchio made inquiry as to whether a warrant or other legal process had been secured in support of that request," [Herbert] Stern said. "When he learned that no such authority had been granted and that there was a disinclination on the part of the authorities to use any legal process, including the Special [FISA] Court which had been established to handle such matters, Mr. Nacchio concluded that these requests violated the privacy requirements of the Telecommunications Act."[45]

Qwest did the right thing, in contrast to AT&T and other companies.

43, 45. Ellen Nakashima and Dan Eggen, "Former CEO Says U.S. Punished Phone Firm." From The Washington Post, Oct. 13, 2007.
© 2007 The Washington Post, All rights reserved. Used by permission and protected by the Copyright Laws of the United States. The printing, copying, redistribution, or retransmission of the Material without express written permission is prohibited.
44. Leslie Cauley, "NSA has massive database of Americans' phone calls," *USA Today*, May 11, 2006

Bush continued to demand more "updates" to FISA, even though Congress passed several more updates to the Patriot Act in the next few years, all giving the government expanded spying powers. Bush himself had given a speech after the initial passage of the Patriot Act in October 2001, praising the Act and saying he now had all the "tools" he needed to protect the country.

The increasing urgency to "update" FISA yet again was spurred by the president's legal vulnerability after it came out that he was doing warrantless eavesdropping. Soon he was pushing for "retroactive immunity" for the telecommunications companies as well as for administration officials who were involved in the NSA spying operation. Ironically, he eventually succeeded only after the Democrats took over Congress, as Glenn Greenwald pointedly commented on Salon.com:

> I'd like to underscore the fact that in 2006, when the Congress was controlled by Bill Frist and Denny Hastert, the administration tried to get a bill passed legalizing warrantless eavesdropping and telecom amnesty, but was unable. They had to wait until the Congress was controlled by Steny Hoyer, Nancy Pelosi and Harry Reid to accomplish that.[46]

The Democrats swept into control of Congress in November 2006, finally breaking the six years of Republican domination of the government. But Democratic House Speaker Nancy Pelosi set the tone when she immediately and gratuitously announced that "impeachment is off the table."

---

46. Glenn Greenwald, "George Bush's latest powers, courtesy of the Democratic Congress," Salon.com, June 19, 2008. Technically speaking, the final bill gave immunity only for the telecoms, but the practical effect was to protect the government by crushing the lawsuits.

Having disarmed themselves, the Democratic leaders spent the next year and a half in pure theater, posturing as opponents of the illegal NSA program while seeking a legal way to protect the president. A handful of evidently sincere defenders of civil liberties, such as Senator Chris Dodd (whose father had been the No. 2 prosecutor at the Nuremberg Nazi war crimes trials), waged a rearguard fight against the warrantless spying, but were hamstrung by their own leadership.

Thus the relevant Intelligence and Judiciary Committees, which were now led by Democrats such as Rockefeller, Feinstein and Leahy in the Senate and John Conyers and Sylvestre Reyes in the House, quickly decided not to launch any serious investigations into the NSA spying, particularly as the White House outrageously refused to hand over any of the relevant records, even the legal opinions on the program. Requests and subpoenas were consistently ignored on the grounds of "executive privilege" and "national security," and Congress declined to press the matter in order to avoid a confrontation.

The very fact that none of the relevant committees ever bothered to contact me, let alone invite me to testify, was an indication that they did not want to seriously probe into the program. If I had been called, that would have upped media interest and better informed the American people about what was going on, and so by their inaction the Democratic Congress was helping the president cover it all up.

In fact, the Democratic Party leaders' collusion with the president was deeper and more direct than I realized at the start of my efforts. Over time, information trickled out that key Democratic leaders had been "briefed" on the NSA spying program very early on and thus were in on the secret but took no action to stop it.

On March 10, 2004, Vice President Dick Cheney convened a secret emergency meeting with top administration security officials including then-NSA Director General Michael Hayden and "the four ranking members of the House and Senate, and the chairmen and vice chairmen of the intelligence committees," according to Barton Gellman in his book, *Angler: The Cheney Vice Presidency* (2008).

Attorney General John Ashcroft, then hospitalized, and his deputy James B. Comey had refused to certify that the warrantless spying program was legal, and Cheney was determined to override their resistance. Attorney General Roberto Gonzales later claimed there was a "consensus in the room," and by his account, says Gellman, "four Democrats and four Republicans, duly informed that the Justice Department had ruled something unlawful, said the White House should do it anyway." Cheney corroborated this account on *Fox News* (Dec. 22, 2008).

Though Democratic leaders have quibbled over exactly what they had been told and what they had said, there's certainly no record of any serious organized opposition. On the Democratic side at this key meeting, the four were then-House Minority Leader Nancy Pelosi, House Intelligence Committee ranking minority member Jane Harman, then-Senate Minority leader Tom Daschle, and ranking minority member of the Senate Intelligence Committee Jay Rockefeller. Later, Rockefeller would become a prime mover in engineering the final amnesty bill for the telecoms in the Senate, and Pelosi together with Steny Hoyer did the same in the House.

As late as the end of 2005 there were "no more than 14 members of Congress" briefed on the program, according to the *New York Times* (Dec. 21, 2005). The list was gradually expanded to include other leaders, so that when the Senate was debating the final "immunity" bill on July 8, 2008, it was revealed that there were indeed a substantial number of members in both houses that had been briefed: "37 members of the Senate," according to Senator Rockefeller, and in the House, "21 House Intelligence Committee members briefed and as many as 40 Judiciary Committee members," according to Senator Specter, who noted that the total amounted to "17.75 percent of the entire Congress."[47]

The Congressional Democratic leaders' silent complicity in the secret program probably goes a long way in explaining their refusal to make a move against the White House, and their push to help the president cover up the illegal program.

The posturing against the NSA spying suddenly collapsed in early August 2007 when, as Congress was rushing to get out of town for summer recess, Speaker Pelosi rammed through the "Protect America Act" (PAA), which basically legalized the illegal program going forward, lacking only the "retroactive immunity" element. Civil liberties groups like the ACLU, who had been cut out of the secret talks, had been stabbed in the back by the Democrats who claimed to be their friend. The PAA was quickly signed by Bush on August 5.

Sensing that the Democrats were in full retreat, Bush now pressed harder to get the missing piece, retroactive immunity for the telecoms. The fight became focused on two bills in the Senate that November.

At this time Kevin Bankston and Cindy Cohn, Legal Director of EFF, invited me to join them in going to Washington for a last-ditch lobbying effort to defeat the Congressional push for telecom immunity. I agreed, and we prepared for another battle.

---

47. Congressional Record, U.S. Senate, July 8, 2008

Chapter 8

"Mr. Klein Goes to Washington"

GOING TO WASHINGTON had some irony for me. Thirty years before, I had been one of hundreds of thousands of Vietnam War protesters marching on the Capitol mall; now I was returning to quietly lobby senators and representatives. I mentioned this amusing contrast to Cindy Cohn, and soon I discovered a lighthearted cartoon posted on the EFF website which evoked James Stewart in the classic movie, "Mr. Smith Goes to Washington" (below). They also produced a color leaflet with a diagram of the splitter apparatus to demonstrate what it was all about for legislators (see next page).

EFF was smart about this campaign. They engaged two professional lobbyists who set up appointments and escorted us around the Capitol building: Adam Eisgrau and former

Graphic by Hugh D'Andrade/eff.org (Creative Commons Attribution-NonCommercial License)

ELECTRONIC FRONTIER FOUNDATION
Protecting Rights and Defending Freedom on the Electronic Frontier

454 SHOTWELL STREET, SAN FRANCISCO, CA, USA   415.436.9333   WWW.EFF.ORG

AT&T's Role in Dragnet Surveillance of Millions of Its Customers

INTERNET SPYING IN SAN FRANCISCO[1]

AT&T's internet traffic in San Francisco runs through fiber-optic cables at an AT&T facility located at 611 Folsom Street in San Francisco. Using a device called a "splitter" a complete copy of the internet traffic that AT&T receives – email, web browsing requests, and other electronic communications sent to or from the customers of AT&T's WorldNet Internet service from people who use another internet service provider – is diverted onto a separate fiber-optic cable which is connected to a room, known as the SG-3 room, which is controlled by the NSA. The other copy of the traffic continues onto the internet to its destination.

The SG-3 room was created under the supervision of the NSA, and contains powerful computer equipment connecting to separate networks. This equipment is designed to analyze communications at high speed, and can be programmed to review and select out the contents and traffic patterns of communications according to user-defined rules. Only personnel with NSA clearances – people assisting or acting on behalf of the NSA – have access to this room.

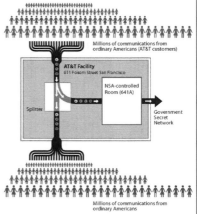

Intercepting Communications at AT&T Folsom Street Facility

AT&T's deployment of NSA-controlled surveillance capability apparently involves considerably more locations than would be required to catch only international traffic. The evidence of the San Francisco room is consistent with an overall national AT&T deployment to from 15 to 20 similar sites, possibly more. This implies that a substantial fraction, probably well over half, of AT&T's purely domestic traffic was diverted to the NSA. At the same time, the equipment in the room is well suited to the capture and analysis of large volumes of data for purposes of surveillance.

---

1 This is a brief summary of the testimony of Mark Klein, a former AT&T technician, and of expert witness J. Scott Marcus, a former Senior Advisor for Internet Technology at the FCC. The complete declaration of Mark Klein is available at http://www.eff.org/legal/cases/att/SER_klein_decl.pdf. The declaration of J. Scott Marcus is available at http://www.eff.org/legal/cases/att/SER_marcus_decl.pdf.

Graphic by Hugh D'Andrade/eff.org. Reprinted by permission.

Electronic Frontier Foundation's flyer for the trip to Washington, D.C.

Congressman Tom Downey. They also hired a professional media company to arrange the publicity and prep us for a well-advertised press conference scheduled for Nov. 7. I must add that Cindy Cohn herself was an amazing organizer of people in a high-pressure situation, constantly on her cell phone or laptop preparing things and rearranging appointments as we scurried through the Congressional hallways and grabbed taxis to be interviewed by news media.

We were joined by Brian Reid, Director of Engineering and Technical Operations at Internet Systems Consortium, which he described in his own EFF leaflet as "a non-profit organization devoted to supporting a non-proprietary Internet." He is a telecommunications and data networking expert who has been involved in the development of several critical Internet technologies, and he generously volunteered his time for this campaign. Reid had been one of the four experts consulted by the *New York Times* to assess the AT&T documents, and he forthrightly told them it was evidence of heavy-duty government spying. He would speak at the Nov. 7 press conference, and as he told me beforehand, "My job is to make people believe you."

Before the week started, we met with the media company to prep our statements for the press conference. I learned something about advertising here. We first submitted our brief statements and they coached us in how to make it something really punchy that gets the message across. My dull, pedantic statement was vastly improved. The key: Limit it to two minutes and *start out* with a numbered list of the points you want to make. That really focuses the mind.

Starting Monday, the week flashed by like a blur as we rushed everywhere trying to be on time for appointments with senators and representatives or their staffs, and various newspeople. I joked to Cindy that I wanted to complain to my shop steward because I wasn't getting a pee break. Our lobbyist allies knew all the key players personally, and as we passed by some of them in the hallways I was introduced, and courtesy required the usual greetings. At one point while in the hallway I found myself shaking the hand of House majority leader Steny Hoyer, who later turned out to be the water boy for the White House's immunity bill. At another point by accident we met Speaker Pelosi in the hallway, and by happenstance she had a photographer with her who snapped our picture. I never saw it and I hope they lost it.

You could count the friendly legislators on one hand. Others just listened, and mostly we could only talk to their staff people. Senator Barbara Boxer invited us to a meeting of her supporters at an apartment in the evening, where she allowed me a few minutes to describe what I knew.

C-SPAN

Senator Chris Dodd speaks on the Senate floor, Dec. 17, 2007.

Congressman Rush Holt sat down with us in his office for a very friendly meeting; he was once a physicist who had actually worked with lasers and beam splitters, so he had a good technical understanding. Pointing to the splitter diagram in the EFF leaflet, he said, *"That* is beyond the pale." I nodded in agreement.

Unfortunately I missed meeting Senator Chris Dodd, who vowed to filibuster any bill with immunity in it. He was out on the campaign trail for his presidential bid, but he arranged for me to meet with his staff so they could make a video interview with me which he posted on his official website.

Dodd stood head and shoulders over the rest of his party because he was not afraid to openly mention my name and describe my specific revelations on the floor of Congress[48]— at the height of his filibuster effort which stalled the immunity bill for months. My jaw dropped when watching C-SPAN at home on December 17, 2007 as Dodd began a comprehensive speech defending Constitutional principles lasting nearly an hour, and behind him someone erected a signboard with my name, photo and blurb on it. He then proceeded to read into the Congressional Record whole sections of my technical statements against the NSA spying program, and paid tribute to me repeatedly as follows:

> The telecoms' 5-year-old program only became public information because there was a whistleblower, Madam President, a gentleman by the name of Mark Klein, who was an employee of AT&T for more than 20 years.
>
> He was really responsible for us being aware of this program. Had it not been for Mark Klein stepping up,

---

48. For the record, Rep. Dennis Kucinich also used my name and information in one of his 35 articles of impeachment against president Bush presented to the House on June 9, 2008. But he was easily overridden by the party leadership, who disappeared his articles in the maw of the Judiciary Committee.

Personal photo of Mark Klein

Press conference, Nov. 7, 2007: Brian Reid, Mark Klein, congressional aide

Personal photo of Mark Klein

Lobbying in Capitol dome, Nov. 7, 2007:
Kevin Bankston, Mark Klein, Brian Reid, Cindy Cohn, Tom Downey

this story might have remained secret for years and years, causing further erosion of our rights. Mark Klein and others were principally responsible for coming forward and expressing their deep concerns.

I think it is important for my colleagues in this body to understand precisely what these telecom communities are doing at the behest of the Bush administration. Mark Klein was courageous enough to blow the whistle on one such program at AT&T's facility at 611 Folsom Street in San Francisco. When the government's warrantless surveillance program came to light in December of 2005, Mr. Klein realized he had unwittingly aided and abetted an extensive, untargeted spying program that may have violated the civil liberties of millions of Americans. In early 2006, Mr. Klein went public with evidence of this program, providing over 100 pages of authenticated schematic diagrams and tables detailing how AT&T diverted its customers' communications to a room controlled by the NSA, with sophisticated equipment inside capable of analyzing millions of customers' Internet activities and e-mails in real time.

But the regular media did not pick up on this speech, and Dodd was run over by his own party leadership on the way to passing the immunity bill.

By the November 7, 2007 press conference, we were already having a snowball effect with the media, including a beautiful spread with pictures that morning on the front page of the business section of the *Washington Post*. Before the conference started, an older woman came up to me and said, "Mr. Klein, I'm a Lucent retiree, and I hate AT&T because they took away my medical care. Can I take my picture with you?" My heart went out to her, and someone took a photo for us.

Cindy Cohn led off the press conference with a sketch of

the lawsuit and why we were in Washington, and then introduced me. I presented my four summary points at the outset:

> 1. AT&T provided the government spy agency with *everything* that ordinary Americans communicated over the Internet: e-mails, text messages, Internet phone calls, web browsing—you name it.

> 2. That specifically and necessarily includes billions of purely *domestic* communications, not just foreign or international communications. This reality directly contradicts President Bush's claim that the government program involved only international communications.

> 3. This program not only included AT&T customers but *everyone who used the Internet,* whether they were AT&T customers or not, because AT&T's network carries messages for many other carriers, such as Sprint and Qwest—they're all connected together to give you the Internet.

> 4. I also know that the secret spy room in San Francisco was not the only such installation: I know of others in Los Angeles, San Diego, Seattle, San Jose, and Atlanta. I have reason to believe that there were 15-20 rooms in total across the country.

Brian Reid added some very damning technical comments about the NSA apparatus which he also detailed in an EFF leaflet. He had reviewed the AT&T documents and asserted forthrightly that "The most likely use of this infrastructure is wholesale, untargeted surveillance of ordinary Americans at the behest of the NSA," and he went on:

AT&T's Setup is Not Appropriate for Targeted or Merely International Surveillance.

This infrastructure is not limited to, nor would it be especially efficient for, targeted surveillance, or even untargeted surveillance aimed at communications where one of the ends is located outside the United States. It is also not reasonably aimed at supporting AT&T operations and security procedures. There are three main reasons:

- **Massive, "Real-Time" Surveillance Capability.** The technological infrastructure is far more powerful and expensive than that needed to do targeted surveillance or surveillance aimed only at international or one-end foreign communications. For example, it includes a NARUS 6400, a computer that can:

  - Simultaneously analyze huge amounts of information based on rules provided by the machine operator.

  - Analyze the content of messages and other information, not just headers or routing information.

  - Conduct the analysis in "real time," rather than after a delay.

  - Correlate information from multiple sources, multiple formats, over many protocols and through different periods of time in that analysis.

- **Capability to Secretly Move Huge Amounts of Data from the facility Elsewhere.** The documents describe a secret, private backbone network separate from the public network where normal AT&T customer traffic is carried. A separate backbone network would not be required for transmission of the smaller amounts of data captured via targeted surveillance. You don't need that magnitude of transport capacity if you are doing targeted surveillance.

- **Downtown San Francisco Location of the Equipment.** The San Francisco facility is not located near an entry/exit point for international communications that happen to be transmitted through the United States, either through undersea cable or via satellite. As a result, it would not be a sensible place to locate a facility aimed at simply monitoring traffic to or from foreign countries.

Later that day, I appeared on MSNBC's *Countdown* show with Keith Olbermann, where I laid out the details of the illegal spying to a nationwide audience. At one point Olbermann asked if my experience felt like "finding yourself in a scene from the sci-fi flick *Invasion of the Body Snatchers*—did it have that sort of horror quality to it?" I replied that "my thought was George Orwell's *1984* and here I am being forced to connect the Big Brother machine." "Oh boy," he said worriedly.

We had an astounding media success, but did it move Congress? Subsequent events suggest that the media spotlight caused them to hesitate, but only for a moment.

Our lobbyist gained my entry to a hearing of the Senate Judiciary Committee the next day, Nov. 8. As we entered the packed room, we saw a crowd of press people lined up against the rear wall. I walked towards them and there were numerous smiling faces of recognition turned towards me. There were no seats available, and as I took my place in the standing crowd, a woman grabbed my arm and whispered in my ear, "God bless you." I sensed this crowd was behind me. Before us was the Judiciary Committee seated around a table in a meeting chaired by Senator Patrick Leahy, and they were all lit up by TV klieg lights.

Senator Feinstein, who had just gotten the Intelligence Committee to pass a bill with immunity in it, was now pushing hard in this committee for the same thing. In her statement to the Judiciary Committee, she outrageously painted the telecom companies as innocent victims who were being "held hostage to costly litigation in what is essentially a complaint about administration activities."[49] With the sympathetic crowd standing around me in the rear of the hearing room, it felt to me like a silent confrontation.

Perhaps because of my presence at this hearing, some newspeople later misreported that I had testified to Congress, but in fact I was never invited to testify for any Congressional committee.

After we left town, the Judiciary Committee passed a bill without immunity. That was a small but ephemeral victory.

Senate Majority Leader Harry Reid now had a choice: He could present the Senate with the Judiciary Committee bill as the "base" bill, which would favor the anti-immunity forces since it is hard to change the base bill; or he could present the Intelligence Committee bill, which would favor the White House. He chose the latter, and the immunity bill was now in play for a vote.

Senator Dodd countered by putting a "hold" on the bill, an act which Majority Leader Reid, following Senate tradition, had always respected whenever a single Republican senator wanted to sideline an especially distasteful bill. But Reid was so anxious to push through the FISA bill that he did not honor the "hold" from a member of his own party, and he scheduled a vote for the week before Christmas.

Dodd evidently regarded this issue as a matter of constitutional principle, so he mounted an actual filibuster with the help of Senator Russ Feingold, and thus on Dec. 17, 2007, he gave a long speech in which he praised me and quoted at length from my technical revelations about the "secret room." As a result of this time-consuming activity, Reid ran

---

49. Bob Egelko, "Feinstein backs legal immunity for telecom firms in wiretap cases," *San Francisco Chronicle*, Nov. 9, 2007

out of time as the year-end holiday recess loomed, and he was forced to postpone action until the following year. In February 2008, with the filibuster forces led by Dodd having been exhausted, Reid forced through the FISA immunity bill.[50]

Everyone now expected the House to collapse in the arms of the Senate as it had the previous August when the PAA was rushed through by Pelosi. But the Speaker chose to protect her turf by refusing to accept the Senate bill and instead fashioned a showpiece FISA bill without immunity in March of 2008. For a couple of months Pelosi basked in the glow of praise from civil liberties groups for her "stand," but it turned out to be only a pose.

Her cohort, House Majority Leader Steny Hoyer, had begun secret negotiations with the White House for another immunity bill, this time with a figleaf fake "concession" which was meant to give the appearance that "judicial review" was being preserved. Pelosi rammed it through the House on June 20 with a vote of 293-129.

The so-called "compromise" *required* the judge to dismiss the lawsuits if the telecoms could show they had a piece of paper showing they had been ordered to assist the NSA and it was claimed to be lawful by the president. The judge would not be allowed to decide on the legality of the order itself; he would be reduced to the role of checking their paperwork, and everyone already knew that such pieces of paper had been given to the telecoms. In effect Congress had endorsed the infamous Nuremberg defense at the postwar trials of Nazi war criminals who said that

---

50. We actually flew back to Washington in Jan. 2008 when Senator Jim Webb (D., VA) asked to see me. But it turned out he was not interested in preventing immunity, and indeed he voted against removing immunity in the final FISA bill passed in July 2008.

they were "just following orders."

This was not a "compromise"—"It is a capitulation," Senator Feingold bitterly commented to TV news on June 19 in a statement later posted on his website. The final battle against the president's immunity maneuver now loomed in the Senate.

Just before the Senate battle, Judge Walker in San Francisco issued his decision in the *Al-Haramain* case, which had been bumped back to him from the Ninth Circuit. It was evident that Walker anticipated which way the wind was blowing and decided to take this last chance to knock out the legal legs from under the government's "state secrets" assertions, even if it was only for the record. Boxed in by the technical restrictions handed down by the higher court, he was forced to dismiss the *Al-Haramain* case, but ruled:

> *FISA preempts the state secrets privilege* in connection with electronic surveillance for intelligence purposes and would appear to displace the state secrets privilege for purposes of plaintiffs' claims. [Emphasis added.][51]

Tipping his cards to the public, Walker suggested in his decision that there was a "rich lode" of public information to back up the plaintiffs' complaint in *Al-Haramain*, even without using the suppressed secret document.

In early January 2009, Judge Walker ruled that there now were "sufficient facts" established in *Al-Haramain* to reinstate the case. But in February the new Obama administration, following exactly in the footsteps of the former Bush regime, invoked the "state secrets" privilege yet again to block the case, only a few days after invoking it in another lawsuit against the CIA's rendition/torture program. Even

---

51. Kurt Opsahl, "Court Holds That FISA Preempts State Secret Privilege," eff.org, July 2, 2008.

after a federal appeals court denied their request for a stay, the new Department of Justice arrogantly defied the judge's order to make the secret document available to the plaintiff's lawyers, and instead challenged the judge's authority to issue such an order. Bush or Obama, no change has happened here.

It was evident that the government would be in deep doo-doo if the telecom lawsuits went forward in Walker's court. And that was the real reason for their desperate push to get immunity.

Chapter 9

"When the President Does It, It's Not Illegal"

IN JULY 2008 I was asked by the Government Accountability Project's Tom Devine in Washington to join in one final media effort to turn the tide in Congress. GAP had been assisting another whistleblower, Babak Pasdar, who had courageously risked his career to expose illegal government spying. As Wired.com's Kevin Poulsen reported:[52]

> A U.S. government office in Quantico, Virginia, has direct, high-speed access to a major wireless carrier's systems, exposing customers' voice calls, data packets and physical movements to uncontrolled surveillance, according to a computer security consultant who says he worked for the carrier in late 2003.
>
> "What I thought was alarming is how this carrier ended up essentially allowing a third party outside their organization to have unfettered access to their environment," Babak Pasdar, now CEO of New York-based Bat Blue told THREAT LEVEL. "I wanted to put some access controls around it; they vehemently denied it. And when I wanted to put some logging around it, they denied that."

Quantico is the home of a Marine base and the FBI's electronic surveillance operations. Pasdar is legally prevented

---

52. Kevin Poulsen, "Whistle-Blower: Feds Have a Backdoor Into Wireless Carrier—Congress Reacts," Wired.com, March 6, 2008. Copyright © 2008 Condé Nast Publications. All rights reserved. Originally published in Wired.com. Reprinted by permission.

from identifying the company, but Poulsen notes his claims are "nearly identical" to those made against Verizon Wireless in a 2006 lawsuit against four companies and the government.

I collaborated with Pasdar on a joint letter opposing FISA immunity which GAP arranged to be commercially distributed to newspapers across the country. But only a few smaller newspapers like the *St. Louis Post-Dispatch* carried it.

As the last fight against FISA immunity approached in early July 2008, numerous civil liberties groups held out a slim hope that Feingold and Dodd would be able to derail the FISA bill yet again. Amy Goodman asked me about this on *Democracy Now!* (July 7, 2008), and I replied:

> Senator Feingold and Senator Dodd have been waging a valiant last-ditch effort to stop this thing. The problem they face is that their own party leadership is against them. This latest bill was rammed through the House by Speaker Pelosi, who had said earlier that she was against immunity, but then she suddenly turned and rammed this through.
>
> And the same thing is happening now in the Senate. And Senator Obama, who a few months ago, before he was the nominee, explicitly said he would not vote for any bill that had immunity in it, and now, a few days ago, he's reversed his position and said he will vote for this bill.
>
> So the Democratic leadership is overriding the fights that Feingold and Dodd are trying to wage, and they're basically carrying out a secret agreement with the White House. Remember, there were never any open hearings on this. They met in secret with the telephone lobbyists and with intelligence agency officials. It was all a secret deal, a conspiracy against the American people. They never had hearings. I was never invited to any hearings. And they're going to ram this through.

The Senate passed the final bill by a wide margin of 69-28 on July 9, and Bush rushed to sign it into law the very next day.

History is marching backwards. The Democratic Party has in effect unwound one of the main reforms[53] of the post-Watergate era and accepted the outrageous criminal rationalizations of Nixon himself. In 1977, just a few years after he had been forced to resign in disgrace, Nixon was interviewed by David Frost, who asked about "wiretappings, burglaries, or so-called black bag jobs." Nixon replied:

> "When the president does it that means that it is not illegal."

This was the essence of the new FISA "compromise." By refusing to enforce the FISA law, by allowing the president to get away with breaking the law, Congress has turned it into a dead letter—and in the process, rubber-stamped the Nixon/Bush doctrine. It is the twisted judicial logic of a dictatorship.

Wiretapping without warrants, denial of *habeas corpus*, torture, secret prisons, wars of aggression—all the crimes long associated with dictatorial regimes are now flaunted by the United States government. The historical "rule of law" which professedly formed the foundation of the Constitution is now openly flouted by the government.

With both parties dealing a death blow to the lawsuits, I felt there should at least be a record of my personal protest,

---

53. "Reform" may be an overstatement in this case: FISA actually institutionalized a secret court with secret hearings at which only the government side could appear—hardly a democratization of government, but the announced intent was to provide a check on the president. In *Mayfield v. United States*, which is still on appeal, a district court ruled that the FISA law itself violates the 4th Amendment by weakening "probable cause" requirements and allowing covert searches.

so I wrote a short statement which I offered to the *New York Times*. They initially expressed some interest, but in the end published nothing. I sent it to Ryan Singel, who used it in a Wired.com/Threat Level story.[54] My concluding paragraph summed up the dark situation:

> The surveillance system now approved by Congress provides the physical apparatus for the government to collect and store a huge database on virtually the entire population, available for data mining whenever the government wants to target its political opponents at any given moment—all in the hands of an unrestrained executive power. It is the infrastructure for a police state.

The fight to defend democratic rights has suffered a very serious defeat. Congress has dealt a blow to the Constitution itself, with both major parties participating in it. And the Democratic Party has basically repudiated its post-Watergate reform posture and embraced Nixon.

The full story has yet to be told. Who exactly is being spied upon? What information on whom is being stored in those huge new NSA data warehouses in Aurora, Colorado and San Antonio, Texas? What was the secret spying activity which the White House was so desperate to get approval for in 2004 that they tried to get then-Attorney General John Ashcroft to sign off on it from his hospital bed, and even *he* refused?

Another aspect of all this which needs further exploration is the complicity of the corporate media in pushing the government's agenda and silencing the critics by omission. For instance, I had personal evidence (chapter 5) of backchannel communications between a certain senator

---

54. Ryan Singel, "AT&T Whistleblower: Spy Bill Creates 'Infrastructure for a Police State'," Wired.com, June 27, 2008

who refused to talk to me and a newspaper which refused to publish my evidence. The two of them apparently had no problems discussing my evidence with each other in private, but deliberately kept it from the public's view—while the paper's "top guy" was discussing the proposed exposé of illegal government surveillance with…the NSA and DNI directors!

And then there is the paper of record which boasts "All the News That's Fit to Print" but sits on a major story about illegal government activity for over a year because they had privately shown it to the government and encountered self-serving objections. I'm sure a lot more of that sort of "old boys club" conferring goes on all the time—essentially an informal mechanism for the government to censor the media, which is all too willing to comply.

The American people should learn the covered-up details of what the government is doing to us. As philosopher George Santayana famously said, "Those who cannot remember the past are condemned to repeat it." That is my reason for writing this book.

FIGHTING BIG BROTHER

Epilogue

Déjà Vu All Over Again

THE U.S. GOVERNMENT INVOKED its new FISA powers against the telecom lawsuits in September 2008. In classic Orwellian doublespeak, Attorney General Michael Mukasey simultaneously denied the government was engaged in any "dragnet" surveillance, and then asked the court for immunity for the telecoms. This was the "certification" called for in the statute passed by Congress in July:[55]

> While confirming the existence of the TSP [Terrorist Surveillance Program], the Government has denied the existence of the alleged dragnet collection on the content of plaintiffs' communications....
>
> As set forth below and in my classified certification, specific information demonstrating that the alleged content dragnet has not occurred cannot be disclosed on the public record without causing exceptional harm to national security. However, because there was no such alleged content-dragnet, no provider participated in that alleged activity. Each of the provider-defendants [AT&T and other telecoms] is therefore entitled to

---

55. "Public Certification of the Attorney General of the United States," filed Sept. 19, 2008

statutory protection with respect to claims based on this allegation pursuant to Section 802(a)(5) of the FISA.

The detailed reasons for protection of each specific company were hidden in a secret filing to the court, so the public would not be told which companies cooperated in the illegal warrantless spying.

The court now had to review the Attorney General's legal filing and, according to the FISA statute, dismiss the lawsuit against AT&T and others if their paperwork was in order. Judge Vaughn Walker set a hearing for December 2.

But the Electronic Frontier Foundation would not give up so easily. In mid-October the EFF and its allies submitted a brief to the court challenging the constitutionality of the new FISA immunity provisions. Accompanying their brief were seven thick binders of exhibits showing just about everything publicly revealed about the massive surveillance programs. Their core argument began:[56]

> The question now before this Court is whether Congress can empower the Executive to exclude the Judiciary from considering the lawfulness of the telecommunications carriers' role in the Executive's well-documented program of warrantless surveillance and, if so, whether the novel and unprecedented scheme set up by section 802 of the Foreign Intelligence Surveillance Act constitutionally accomplishes this exclusion. At stake are the privacy rights of every American who trusts and uses the communication facilities of AT&T, MCI, Verizon, BellSouth, Cingular, or Sprint to transmit their most private and important thoughts. But also at stake is something equally fundamental—the role of the Judiciary in the constitutional structure of our government. For if Congress can give

---

56. "MDL Plaintiffs' Opposition to Motion of the United States Seeking to Apply 50 U.S.C. § 1885a To Dismiss These Actions," filed Oct. 17, 2008

the Executive the power to exclude the Judiciary from considering the constitutional claims of millions of Americans, can abdicate to the Executive the authority to change the law applicable in specific litigation, and can prevent the Judiciary from making an independent determination of the facts and law in specific litigation, then the Judiciary will no longer be functioning as a co-equal branch of government.

On September 18 the EFF also filed a new lawsuit aimed directly at the NSA, President Bush, Vice President Cheney and their cohorts in the administration. This opened a "second front," they said, as described in their press release:

The lawsuit, *Jewel v. NSA*, is aimed at ending the NSA's dragnet surveillance of millions of ordinary Americans and holding accountable the government officials who illegally authorized it. Evidence in the case includes undisputed documents provided by former AT&T telecommunications technician Mark Klein showing AT&T has routed copies of Internet traffic to a secret room in San Francisco controlled by the NSA.

The day before the Dec. 2 hearing in *Hepting v. AT&T* and related cases, Judge Walker gave a hint of his thinking by issuing a list of eleven pointed questions directed toward both sides. In the second question he asked:

What exactly has Congress created with § 802 [the new FISA amendment of 2008]? It does not appear to be an affirmative defense but rather appears to be a retroactive immunity for completed acts that allegedly violated constitutional rights, but one that can only be activated by the executive branch. Is there any precedent for this type of enactment that is analogous in all of these respects: retroactivity; immunity for constitutional violations; and delegation of broad discretion to the executive branch to determine whether to invoke the provision?

This key legal question became the focus of the hearing.

Judge Walker announced at the beginning that he had not read the government's latest classified filings because he wanted to rely only on the public arguments. "What has been filed in the public record is all that I have seen,"[57] he emphasized, apparently reflecting his distaste for secret government briefs which the plaintiffs are barred from reviewing—a blatant violation of due process.

The U.S. Department of Justice's Principal Deputy Associate Attorney General Carl Nichols began to present his arguments for dismissal of the lawsuits but could get out only a few words before Judge Walker interrupted him to say that a new Attorney General is about to take office with the administration of President Barack Obama, so "Why shouldn't I just wait to see what the new Attorney General is going to do?" The question he posed, and some civil liberties people were asking, was whether the new administration will simply take up where the old one left off and use the unconstitutional immunity law to thwart the lawsuits, or change course by allowing the cases against the telecoms to go forward?

That question rightly put Obama on the spot, since he had originally opposed immunity but backtracked in the end to help pass the final FISA bill in July 2008. But all hope that he will reverse course yet again and "do the right thing" is wishful thinking.

The election is over, and Obama's cabinet appointments and speeches since then make it clear that his administration is far more about continuity than "change," as was first indicated by his retention of Bush's Secretary of Defense Robert Gates.

Government attorney Nichols told the judge he did not

---

57. Quotes from my personal notes taken at the hearing

expect the new administration to reverse the DOJ's course, but Judge Walker challenged him by posing the question, "What other statute is there that's quite like this statute?" Nichols confessed that he did not think there was one quite like it, and Walker interjected that it was a *"sui generis"* (unique) statute, one which gives the Attorney General *"carte blanche* to immunize anyone."

Attorney Richard Wiebe presented the EFF case, arguing that the government was trying to "immunize untargeted mass warrantless surveillance." When Judge Walker suggested in devil's advocate fashion that perhaps the "remedy" should be directed at the government instead of the telecom carriers, Wiebe noted that the "participation of the carriers is essential in order to complete the surveillance," i.e., the carriers are the "gatekeepers," and so going after the carriers is more "efficacious."

To this Judge Walker snapped back, "I'm the wrong person to be making that argument to—Talk to Senator Feinstein!" Indeed, it was Feinstein who led the charge in protecting the telecoms from the lawsuits, while unhelpfully suggesting that civil liberties groups go sue the government—a nearly impossible task, as the senator knows full well, since the government is qualitatively better armored against lawsuits than private companies.

Governments generally take special care to make it virtually impossible for the commoners to turn the law against the state itself. Judge Walker perhaps unintentionally hinted at this general rule when, in an attempt to counter EFF attorney Cindy Cohn's arguments against immunity for the telecoms, he noted that there is precedent since there are already many immunities written into the law for police and judges.

But the new precedent giving immunity to *private* agents and companies acting at the government's behest only makes the government more dangerous, by enabling it to arbitrarily commit illegal and unconstitutional acts using people who are exempted from the law. That is a characteristic of naked dictatorship.

Near the end of the Dec. 2 hearing, when the judge was trying to figure out to what extent he could review the facts in the case given the new FISA law, a telecom attorney helpfully explained that the law allows the judge to perform an "independent review" but must give "deference" to the executive branch in matters of national security. Walker responded with sarcasm, "Meaningful but restrained review —that certainly clears things up!," which triggered a wave of laughter in the courtroom.

Upon taking the reins of power in 2009, the new Obama administration quickly stepped into the shoes of the former Bush regime without hesitation. Three weeks after his appointment was confirmed by the Senate, the new Attorney General Eric Holder's Department of Justice submitted a supplemental brief to Judge Walker's court on Feb. 25 stating that the former "Attorney General's certification complies with the [FISA] statute" and "Accordingly, the Court should now promptly dismiss these actions" against the phone companies. And again on April 3 the Obama administration invoked "state secrets" to demand dismissal of EFF's lawsuit against the NSA. That's what they call a "seamless transition"!

EFF's Kevin Bankston commented that "it feels like déjà vu all over again." What's more, the Obama DOJ added a new argument never before invoked by the Bush administration: "sovereign immunity," claiming the Patriot Act says the government *can never be sued* for illegal surveillance unless there was "willful disclosure" of the intercepted communications.

As Glenn Greenwald has highlighted,[58] the immunity bill for telecoms was pushed through with assurances by leading Democrats like Senator Rockefeller, who had made a point of noting the bill did not give immunity to government officials but only to the telecoms, and so "lawsuits against the government can go forward." Senator Feinstein also made suggestions that the government, not the telecoms, should be the target of lawsuits.

Thus the omission of government immunity from the telecom bill gave the appearance of a concession, a promise of future "accountability," but it was only a clever ruse. The Democratic leaders must have known the government already had "sovereign immunity" via the Patriot Act, passed with Democratic votes earlier in the Bush administration. Obama used his civil liberties cloak to help him get elected, but now feels free to remove it and cater to the intelligence bureaucracy. It was pure political deception.[59]

On June 3, 2009, Judge Walker dismissed the dozens of remaining lawsuits against all the telecoms including AT&T, arguing that they had valid immunity under the revised FISA law. While EFF and the ACLU are planning a long-shot appeal, the government has no doubt struck a major blow to the Constitution. The blame for this defeat must be directed at both parties, Republican and Democratic.

Congress has ensured that the extensive infrastructure for illegal NSA spying remains in place and in operation.

And there have been indications that it has expanded since my retirement. In December 2004 I was told by a

---

58. Glenn Greenwald, "New and worse secrecy and immunity claims from the Obama DOJ," Salon.com, Apr. 6, 2009

59. In May 2009 in another reversal, Obama also decided to continue the kangaroo-court military commissions at Guantánamo, while refusing to release still-secret photographic evidence of torture.

reliable source that more Lucent patch panels were being installed at Folsom St. so that the splitter cabinet on the 7th floor could accommodate more data circuits to be copied into the secret room on the 6th floor.

Now in 2009 I have heard from another trusted source that the 7th floor itself has become a "secret floor": The floor is *"secured at the elevator"* and *"You can't get off on that floor unless you got a special key."*

Experience has shown that defenders of civil liberties and the Constitution cannot rely on the unverifiable assurances of government officials who hide their practices behind a wall of secrecy. As intrepid reporter I.F. Stone wrote long ago after covering Washington for decades from FDR to LBJ: "All governments lie."[60]

So long as the hardware of the "secret rooms" is in place, the government has a dangerous new power of surveillance. The only surefire restraint on illegal government spying would be the *physical removal* of the secret rooms, splitters and related equipment which enables automated, dragnet surveillance of people's communications on the Internet without warrants. When government has easy access to such an intrusive surveillance apparatus, you can be sure it will be used and abused.

---

60. I.F. Stone, *In a Time of Torment: 1961-67*, p. 317. The full quote is: "All governments lie, but disaster lies in wait for countries whose officials smoke the same hashish they give out."

Appendix A

This appendix contains the original text of my 2004 memo, plus the eight pages of documents released by the court and AT&T (the engineer's personal contact information was redacted). I have omitted the supplemental pages about the Narus which were included in my original PDF version.

The original PDF was posted on Wired.com for several years, but could not be found recently. However, one can still find it in the Internet Archive at *archive.org* by using the "Take Me Back" function to search for the original Wired webpage:

blog.wired.com/27bstroke6/att_klein_wired.pdf

The PDF has the original 2005 cover page title, "AT&T's Implementation of NSA Spying on American Citizens."

—Mark Klein, June 7, 2009

AT&T Deploys Government Spy Gear on WorldNet Network

—16 January, 2004

In 2003 AT&T built "secret rooms" hidden deep in the bowels of its central offices in various cities, housing computer gear for a government spy operation which taps into the company's popular WorldNet service and the entire Internet. These installations enable the government to look at *every individual message* on the Internet and analyze exactly what people are doing. Documents showing the hardwire installation in San Francisco suggest that there are similar locations being installed in numerous other cities.

The physical arrangement, the timing of its construction, the government-imposed secrecy surrounding it, and other factors all strongly suggest that its origins are rooted in the Defense Department's "Total Information Awareness" (TIA) program which brought forth vigorous protests from defenders of Constitutionally-protected civil liberties last year:

> "As the director of the effort, Vice Adm. John M. Poindexter, has described the system in Pentagon documents and in speeches, it will provide intelligence analysts and law enforcement officials with instant access to information from Internet mail and calling records to credit card and banking transactions and travel documents, without a search warrant."
> —*The New York Times*, 9 November 2002

To mollify critics, the Defense Advanced Research Projects Agency (DARPA) spokesmen have repeatedly asserted that they are only conducting "research" using "artificial synthetic data" or information from "normal DoD intelligence channels" and hence there are "no U.S. citizen privacy implications" (Department of Defense, Office of the Inspector General report on TIA, December 12, 2003). They also changed the name of the program to "Terrorism Information Awareness" to make it more politically palatable. But feeling the heat, Congress made a big show of allegedly cutting off funding for TIA in late 2003, and the political fallout resulted in Admiral Poindexter's abrupt resignation last August. However, the fine print reveals that Congress eliminated funding only for "the majority of the TIA components," allowing several "components" to continue (DoD, *ibid.*). The essential hardware elements of a TIA-type spy program are being surreptitiously slipped into "real world" telecommunications offices.

In San Francisco the "secret room" is Room 641A at 611 Folsom Street, the site of a large SBC phone building, three floors of which are occupied by AT&T. High speed fiber optic circuits come in on the 8th floor and run down to the 7th floor where they connect to routers for AT&T's WorldNet service, part of the latter's vital "Common Backbone." In order to snoop on these circuits, a special cabinet was installed and cabled to the "secret room" on the 6th floor to monitor the information going through the circuits. (The location code of the cabinet is 070177.04, which denotes the 7th floor, aisle 177 and bay 04.) The "secret room" itself is roughly 24-by-48 feet, containing perhaps a dozen cabinets including such equipment as Sun servers and two Juniper routers, plus an industrial-size air conditioner.

The normal workforce of unionized technicians in the office are forbidden to enter the "secret room," which has a special combination lock on the main door. The telltale sign of an illicit government spy operation is the fact that *only people with security clearance from the National Security Agency can enter this room.* In practice this has meant that only one management-level technician works in there. Ironically, the one who set up the room was laid off in late 2003 in one of the company's endless "downsizings," but he was quickly replaced by another.

Plans for the "secret room" were fully drawn up by December 2002, curiously only four months after DARPA started awarding contracts for TIA. One 60-page document, identified as coming from "AT&T Labs Connectivity & Net Services" and authored by the labs' consultant Mathew F. Casamassima, is titled "Study Group 3, LGX/Splitter Wiring, San Francisco,"and dated 12/10/02 [see pp. 126-129]. This document addresses the special problem of trying to spy on fiber optic circuits. Unlike copper wire circuits which emit electromagnetic fields that can be tapped into without disturbing the circuits, fiber optic circuits do not "leak" their light signals. In order to monitor such communications, one has to physically cut into the fiber somehow and divert a portion of the light signal to see the information.

This problem is solved with "splitters" which literally split off a percentage of the light signal so it can be examined. This is the purpose of the special cabinet referred to above: circuits are connected into it, the light signal is split into two signals, one of which is diverted to the "secret room." The cabinet is totally unnecessary for the circuit to perform—in fact it introduces problems since the signal level is reduced by the splitter—*its only purpose is to enable a third party to examine the data flowing between sender and recipient on the Internet.*

The above-referenced document includes a diagram [p. 128] showing the splitting of the light signal, a portion of which is diverted to "SG3 Secure Room," i.e., the so-called "Study Group" spy room. Another page headlined "Cabinet Naming" [p. 127] lists not only the "splitter" cabinet but also the equipment installed in the "SG3" room, including various Sun devices, and Juniper M40e and M160 "backbone" routers. [Page 129] shows one of many tables detailing the connections between the "splitter" cabinet on the 7th floor (location 070177.04) and a cabinet in the "secret room" on the 6th floor (location 060903.01). Since the San Francisco "secret room" is numbered 3, the implication is that there are at least several more in other cities (Seattle, San Jose, Los Angeles and San Diego are some of the rumored locations), which likely are spread across the U.S.

One of the devices in the "Cabinet Naming" list is particularly revealing as to the purpose of the "secret room": a Narus STA 6400. Narus is a 7-year-old company which, because of its particular niche, appeals not only to businessmen (it is backed by AT&T, JP Morgan and Intel, among others) but also to police, military and intelligence officials. Last November 13-14, for instance, Narus was the "Lead Sponsor" for a technical conference held in McLean, Virginia, titled "Intelligence Support Systems for Lawful Interception and Internet Surveillance."* Police officials, FBI and DEA agents, and major telecommunications companies eager to cash in on the "war on terror" had gathered in the hometown of the CIA to discuss their special problems. Among the attendees were AT&T, BellSouth, MCI, Sprint and Verizon. Narus founder, Dr. Ori Cohen, gave a keynote speech. So what does the Narus STA 6400 do?

"The [Narus] STA Platform consists of standalone traffic analyzers that collect network and customer usage information in real time directly from the message.... These analyzers sit on the message pipe into the ISP [Internet Service Provider] cloud rather than tap into each router or ISP

---

* TeleStrategies postings, see:
http://www.serviceprovidersclub.com/main/eventdetail.cfm?eventId=36&v=
  agenda
http://telestrategies.com/issworld/sponsors.htm
http://telestrategies.com/iss_2004/index.htm

device" (*Telecommunications* magazine, April, 2000).** A Narus press release (1 Dec., 1999) also boasts that its Semantic Traffic Analysis (STA) technology "captures comprehensive customer usage data…and transforms it into actionable information…[it] is the only technology that provides complete visibility for all Internet applications."***

To implement this scheme, WorldNet's highspeed data circuits already in service had to be re-routed to go through the special "splitter" cabinet. This was addressed in another document of 44 pages from AT&T Labs, titled "<u>SIMS, Splitter Cut-In and Test Procedure</u>," dated 01/13/03 [pp. 130-131]. "SIMS" is an unexplained reference to the secret room. Part of this reads as follows:

> **"A WMS [work] Ticket will be issued by the AT&T Bridgeton Network Operation Center (NOC) to charge time for performing the work described in this procedure document….**
>
> "This procedure covers the steps required to insert optical splitters into select live Common Backbone (CBB) OC3, OC12 and OC48 optical circuits."

The NOC referred to is in Bridgeton, Missouri, and controls WorldNet operations. (As a sign that government spying goes hand-in-hand with union-busting, the entire CWA Local 6377 which had jurisdiction over the Bridgeton NOC was wiped out in early 2002 when AT&T fired the union workforce and later re-hired them as non-union "management" employees.) The cut-in work was performed in 2003, and since then new circuits are connected through the "splitter" cabinet.

Another "Cut-In and Test Procedure" document dated January 24, 2003, provides diagrams of how AT&T Core Network circuits were to be run through the "splitter" cabinet

---

** *see http://www.findarticles.com/cf_dls/m0TLC/4_34/62350496/p1/article.jhtml*
*** *see http://www.lucent.com/press/1299/991201.nsa.html*

[p.132]. One page lists the circuit IDs of key Peering Links which were "cut-in" in February 2003 [p. 133], including ConXion, Verio, XO, Genuity, Qwest, PAIX, Allegiance, Abovenet, Global Crossing, C&W, UUNET, Level 3, Sprint, Telia, PSINet, and Mae West. By the way, Mae West is one of two key Internet nodal points in the United States (the other, Mae East, is in Vienna, Virginia). It's not just WorldNet customers who are being spied on—it's the entire Internet.

The next logical question is, what central command is collecting the data sent by the various "secret rooms"? One can only make educated guesses, but perhaps the answer was inadvertently given in the DoD Inspector General's report (cited above):

> "For testing TIA capabilities, DARPA and the U.S. Army Intelligence and Security Command (INSCOM) created an operational research and development environment that uses real time feedback. The main node of TIA is located at INSCOM [in Fort Belvoir, Virginia]..."

Among the agencies participating or planning to participate in the INSCOM "testing" are the "National Security Agency, the Defense Intelligence Agency, the Central Intelligence Agency, the DoD Counterintelligence Field Activity, the U.S. Strategic Command, the Special Operations Command, the Joint Forces Command and the Joint Warfare Analysis Center." There are also "discussions" going on to bring in "non-DoD Federal agencies" such as the FBI.

This is the infrastructure for an Orwellian police state. It must be shut down!

PERSONAL INFORMATION REDACTED FROM THIS PAGE

Labs Connectivity & Net Services

Study Group 3
LGX/Splitter Wiring
San Francisco

Issue 1, 12/10/02

Author: Mathew F. Casamassima

KLEIN C-1

PERSONAL INFORMATION REDACTED FROM THIS PAGE

Study Group 3 LGX/Splitter Wiring, San Francisco
Issue 1, 12/10/02
Mathew F. Casamassima,

Cabinet Naming:

Equipment	Name
Splitter Cabinet	SPC
LGX Cabinet	LXC
Meta Data Cabinet	MDC
Network Management Cabinet	NMC
Data Filter Cabinet	DFC
Juniper M40E Router Cabinet	JC
Sun V880 Cabinet	S8C
Sun 3800 Cabinet	S3C
Sun Storedge Cabinet	SSC
ADC Chassis For LGX	lxp
ADC Chassis For Splitter	spp
ADC Splitter Module	spl
ADC Bulkhead Module (LGX)	bk
Juniper M160	jp
Juniper M40e	j4
Narus STA 6400	nr
Sun Fire V880/Narus Logic Server	s8
Sun Fire 3800	s3
Sun StorEdge T3	st
Sun StorEdge FC switch	sf
Cisco Catalyst 2924M-XL	cz
BayTech DS9	b9
BayTech RPC22	bv
Brocade SilkWorm 2800 Switch	bz
Lucent LGX	LLGX

PERSONAL INFORMATION REDACTED FROM THIS PAGE

Study Group 3 LGX/Splitter Wiring, San Francisco
Issue 1, 12/10/02
Mathew F. Casamassima,

Splitter to SG3 LGX Connectivity

The Tables in this section give the splitter to SG3 LGX connectivity as shown with in the bounds of this box.

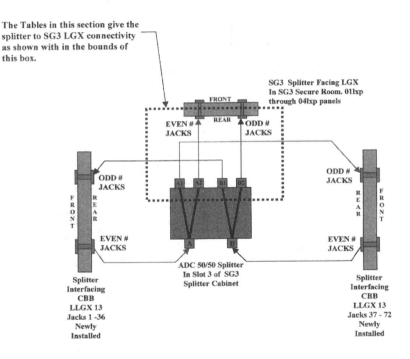

SG3 Splitter Facing LGX
In SG3 Secure Room. 01lxp
through 04lxp panels

FRONT
REAR
EVEN # JACKS
ODD # JACKS

ODD # JACKS
FRONT
REAR
EVEN # JACKS

ODD # JACKS
REAR
FRONT
EVEN # JACKS

ADC 50/50 Splitter
In Slot 3 of SG3
Splitter Cabinet

Splitter
Interfacing
CBB
LLGX 13
Jacks 1 -36
Newly
Installed

Splitter
Interfacing
CBB
LLGX 13
Jacks 37 - 72
Newly
Installed

PERSONAL INFORMATION REDACTED FROM THIS PAGE

Study Group 3 LGX/Splitter Wiring, San Francisco
Issue 1, 12/10/02
Mathew F. Casamassima,

01lxp SG3 LGX Panel to Splitter Cabinet Connectivity

01lxp SG3 LGX Panel Port (In SG3 Room)	Splitter Cabinet Destination	SG3 LGX Designation Card Text	Splitter End Fiber Label Text
1	01spp/Slot 3/port 14	RR 070177.04 01spp/Slot 3/port 14	FROM: 060903.01 01lxp/JK 1 TO: 01spp/Slot 3/port 14
2	01spp/Slot 3/port 13	RR 070177.04 01spp/Slot 3/port 13	FROM: 060903.01 01lxp/JK 2 TO: 01spp/Slot 3/port 13
3	01spp/Slot 3/port 16	RR 070177.04 01spp/Slot 3/port 16	FROM: 060903.01 01lxp/JK 3 TO: 01spp/Slot 3/port 16
4	01spp/Slot 3/port 15	RR 070177.04 01spp/Slot 3/port 15	FROM: 060903.01 01lxp/JK 4 TO: 01spp/Slot 3/port 15
5	01spp/Slot 3/port 18	RR 070177.04 01spp/Slot 3/port 18	FROM: 060903.01 01lxp/JK 5 TO: 01spp/Slot 3/port 18
6	01spp/Slot 3/port 17	RR 070177.04 01spp/Slot 3/port 17	FROM: 060903.01 01lxp/JK 6 TO: 01spp/Slot 3/port 17
7	01spp/Slot 4/port 20	RR 070177.04 01spp/Slot 4/port 20	FROM: 060903.01 01lxp/JK 7 TO: 01spp/Slot 3/port 20
8	01spp/Slot 4/port 19	RR 070177.04 01spp/Slot 4/port 19	FROM: 060903.01 01lxp/JK 8 TO: 01spp/Slot 3/port 19
9	01spp/Slot 4/port 22	RR 070177.04 01spp/Slot 4/port 22	FROM: 060903.01 01lxp/JK 9 TO: 01spp/Slot 3/port 22
10	01spp/Slot 4/port 21	RR 070177.04 01spp/Slot 4/port 21	FROM: 060903.01 01lxp/JK 10 TO: 01spp/Slot 3/port 21
11	01spp/Slot 4/port 24	RR 070177.04 01spp/Slot 4/port 24	FROM: 060903.01 01lxp/JK 11 TO: 01spp/Slot 3/port 24
12	01spp/Slot 4/port 23	RR 070177.04 01spp/Slot 4/port 23	FROM: 060903.01 01lxp/JK 12 TO: 01spp/Slot 3/port 23
13	01spp/Slot 5/port B2	RR 070177.04 01spp/Slot 5/port B2	FROM: 060903.01 01lxp/JK 13 TO:01spp/Slot 5/port B2
14	01spp/Slot 5/port A2	RR 070177.04 01spp/Slot 5/port A2	FROM: 060903.01 01lxp/JK 14 TO:01spp/Slot 5/port A2
15	01spp/Slot 6/port B2	RR 070177.04 01spp/Slot 6/port B2	FROM: 060903.01 01lxp/JK 15 TO:01spp/Slot 6/port B2
16	01spp/Slot 6/port A2	RR 070177.04 01spp/Slot 6/port A2	FROM: 060903.01 01lxp/JK 16 TO:01spp/Slot 6/port A2

KLEIN C-45

Labs Connectivity & Net Services

SIMS
Splitter Cut-In and Test Procedure

Issue 2, 01/13/03

Author: Mathew F. Casamassima

KLEIN A-1

PERSONAL INFORMATION REDACTED FROM THIS PAGE

SIMS - Splitter Test and Cut-In Procedure
Issue 2, 01/13/03
Mathew F. Casamassima,

1. *Procedure Overview*

A WMS Ticket will be issued by the AT&T Bridgeton Network Operation Center (NOC) to charge time for performing the work described in this procedure document. At some point prior to the splitter cut-in being performed your office will be contacted by the Bridgeton Network Operations Center (NOC) to confirm the WMS Ticket has been received. Bridgeton NOC personnel will again contact OSWF the night of the cut to begin coordination. The work described in the procedure will be supported, on-site, by an IP Field Support Specialist (FSS) from the Day Tech organization.

This procedure covers the steps required to insert optical splitters into select live Common Backbone (CBB) OC3, OC12 and OC48 optical circuits. The splitter insertion will be accomplished by removing existing optical cross-connects and installing new cross-connects all within the CBB LGX complex. The optical splitters will be contained in a standalone cabinet located in the proximity of the CBB LGX complex. The splitters will be pre-cabled by an EF&I vendor to the rear of a dedicated LGX bay (LLGX13) within the CBB LGX complex. A partial installation and test of cross-connects can be done prior to the actual splitter cut-in. This portion of the work can be done outside the CBB maintenance window. An IP FSS member of the Day Tech organization will contact OSWF to schedule the pre-cut portion of the work. Section 2 of this document will describe the pre-cut installation of cross-connects and the pre-cut testing of the new circuit path. The actual cut-in of the splitter will be done during the CBB maintenance window and will be closely coordinated with the Bridge NOC and will be supported, on-site, by an IP FSS member of the Day Tech organization. The actual splitter cut-in is described in Section 3 of this document.

The number of cross-connects required and the final path the circuit will take is dependant on the location of the affected LGX bays within the multiple line-ups of the CBB LGX complex. This procedure will describe all possible splitter cut-in circuit paths. The procedure will also describe the procedures for testing each possible circuit path.

1.1. How to Use this Procedure

This procedure document is quite long. It is not necessary to read this whole document to do the work. There are 4 possible LGX arrange that may encounter. By reading section 1.2 below, determine which LGX arrangement applies to the circuit you are working. Then, after reading the introductory paragraphs in Sections 2 and 3, go directly to the subsections within Sections 2 and 3 associated with the LGX arrangement you are dealing with.

1.2. LGX Definition and LGX-Arrangement:

LGX Definition: There are multiple LGX bays affected by this procedure. Within the CBB LGX complex LGX bays follow a specific naming convention (LLGX 1, LLGX2, LLGX3, LLGX4, ...). This naming convention is uniform across sites. Since this document is designed to cover all sites, this uniform naming convention will be used here. Site-specific engineering will use the LGX FIC code rather than the naming. Prior to the start of the work described here the local IP FSS will label the LGX bays with the naming as presented in this document. The following are generic definitions for the LGX bays affected by this procedure:

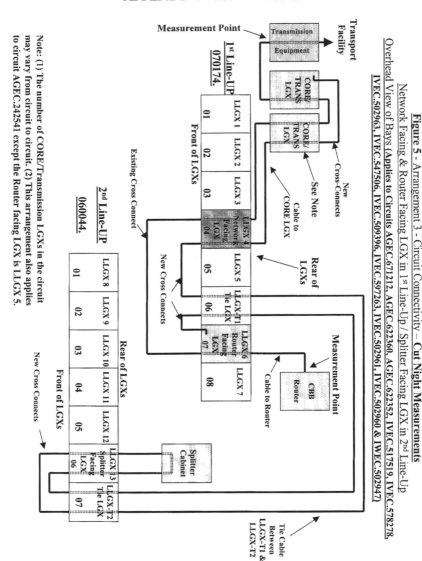

Figure 5 - Arrangement 3 - Circuit Connectivity – **Cut Night Measurements**

Network Facing & Router Facing LGX in 1st Line-Up / Splitter Facing LGX in 2nd Line-Up

Overhead View of Bays (Applies to Circuits AGEC.671212, AGEC.62360, AGEC.62352, IVEC.517519, IVEC.578278, IVEC.502963, IVEC.547506, IVEC.509396, IVEC.597263, IVEC.502961, IVEC.502960 & IWEC.502947)

Note: (1) The number of CORE/Transmission LGXs in the circuit may vary from circuit to circuit. (2) This arrangement also applies to circuit AGEC.242541 except the Router facing LGX is LLGX 5.

Priority	Peering Link	Ckt Type	ID	AS Number	Circuit Comments	Router	Port	Circuit Engineering Change Order Issue Date	Circuit Engineering Complete Date Requested	Circuit Engineering Complete Date Actual	Splitter Pre-Test Date	Splitter in Circuit Date	Splitter Active Date	Comments
1	ConXion	OC-3	AGEC.622352	4544		sffca01ck	POS 1/3	1/22/2003	1/31/2003	1/22/2003	2/4/2003	2/6/2003		
2	Verio	OC-12	IVEC.517519	2914		sffca01ck	POS 3/1	1/23/2003	1/31/2003	1/23/2003	2/4/2003	2/6/2003		
3	XO	OC-12	IVEC.578278	2828		sffca01ck	POS 3/2	1/23/2003	1/31/2003	1/23/2003	2/4/2003	2/6/2003		
4	Genuity	OC-12	IVEC.502963	1		sffca01ck	POS 3/3	1/23/2003	1/31/2003	1/23/2003	2/4/2003	2/6/2003		
5	Qwest	OC-12	IVEC.547606	209		sffca01ck	POS 5/2	1/30/2003	2/7/2003	1/23/2003	2/11/2003	2/13/2003		
6	PAIX	OC-12	IVEC.509396	nap		sffca01ck	POS 8/1	1/30/2003	2/7/2003	1/23/2003	2/11/2003	2/13/2003		
7	Allegiance	OC-12	IVEC.597263	2548		sffca01ck	POS 8/3	1/30/2003	2/7/2003	1/23/2003	2/11/2003	2/13/2003		
8	Abovenet	OC-12	IVEC.502961	6461		sffca01ck	POS 9/2	1/30/2003	2/7/2003	1/24/2003	2/11/2003	2/13/2003		
9	Global Crossing	OC-12	IVEC.502980	3549		sffca01ck	POS 9/3	1/30/2003	2/7/2003	1/24/2003	2/11/2003	2/13/2003		
10	C&W	OC-48	IVEC.502947	3561		sffca01ck	POS 2/0		2/14/2003	2/14/2003	2/18/2003	2/20/2003		
11	UUNET	OC-48	IVEC.509433	701		sffca02ck4	POS 2/0		2/14/2003	2/14/2003	2/18/2003	2/20/2003		
12	Level 3	OC-48	IVEC.509434	3356		sffca02ck4	POS 3/0		2/14/2003	2/14/2003	2/18/2003	2/20/2003		
13	Sprint	OC-48	IVEC.509438	1239		sffca02ck4	POS 11/0		2/21/2003	2/21/2003	2/25/2003	2/27/2003		
14	Telia	OC-3	AGEC.671212	1299		sffca01ck	POS 0/1		2/21/2003	2/21/2003	2/25/2003	2/27/2003		
15	PSINet	OC-3	AGEC.622360	174		sffca01ck	POS 0/2		2/21/2003	2/21/2003	2/25/2003	2/27/2003		
16	Mae West	OC-3	AGEC.242541	nap		sffca02ck	POS 2/5		2/21/2003	2/21/2003	2/25/2003	2/27/2003		

Appendix B

Declaration of Mark Klein

March 28, 2006

Submitted by Mark Klein to the U.S. District Court, Northern District of California, Judge Vaughn Walker presiding, in the case of *Hepting v. AT&T*

1 ELECTRONIC FRONTIER FOUNDATION
   CINDY COHN (145997)
2 cindy@eff.org
   LEE TIEN (148216)
3 tien@eff.org
   KURT OPSAHL (191303)
4 kurt@eff.org
   KEVIN S. BANKSTON (217026)
5 bankston@eff.org
   CORYNNE MCSHERRY (221504)
6 corynne@eff.org
   JAMES S. TYRE (083117)
7 jstyre@eff.org
   454 Shotwell Street
8 San Francisco, CA 94110
   Telephone: 415/436-9333
9 415/436-9993 (fax)

10 TRABER & VOORHEES
   BERT VOORHEES (137623)
11 bv@tvlegal.com
   THERESA M. TRABER (116305)
12 tmt@tvlegal.com
   128 North Fair Oaks Avenue, Suite 204
13 Pasadena, CA 91103
   Telephone: 626/585-9611
14 626/ 577-7079 (fax)
   Attorneys for Plaintiffs
15
   [Additional counsel appear following the signature page.]
16

17   UNITED STATES DISTRICT COURT

18   NORTHERN DISTRICT OF CALIFORNIA

19
   TASH HEPTING, GREGORY HICKS,   )   No. C-06-0672-VRW
20 CAROLYN JEWEL and ERIK KNUTZEN on)
   Behalf of Themselves and All Others Similarly)   CLASS ACTION
21 Situated,   )
)   DECLARATION OF MARK KLEIN IN
22   Plaintiffs,   )   SUPPORT OF PLAINTIFFS' MOTION FOR
)   PRELIMINARY INJUNCTION
23   vs.   )
)   Date: June 8, 2006
24 AT&T CORP., AT&T INC. and DOES 1-20,)   Time: 2:00 p.m.
   inclusive,   )   Court: Courtroom 6, 17th Floor
25   )   Judge: The Hon. Vaughn R. Walker,
              Defendants.   )   Chief United States District Judge
26 _____)

27

28   **FILED UNDER SEAL PURSUANT TO CIVIL LOCAL RULE 79-S**

   DECLARATION OF MARK KLEIN
   C-06-0672-VRW   - 1 -

APPENDIX B: DECLARATION

I, Mark Klein, declare under penalty of perjury that the following is true and correct:

1.   I am submitting this Declaration in support of Plaintiffs' Motion for a Preliminary Injunction. I have personal knowledge of the facts stated herein, unless stated on information and belief, and if called upon to testify to those facts I could and would competently do so.

2.   For over 22 years I worked as a technician for AT&T Corporation ("AT&T"), first in New York and then in California. I started working for AT&T in November 1981 as a Communications Technician.

3.   From January 1998 to October 2003, I worked as a Computer Network Associate III at an AT&T facility on Geary Street in San Francisco, CA.

4.   From October 2003 to May 2004 I worked as a Communications Technician at an AT&T facility at 611 Folsom St., San Francisco, CA (the "Folsom Street Facility").

5.   Previously, I worked as an AT&T Communications Technician from November 1981 to January 1998. I was assigned to AT&T facilities in New York, New York (November 1981 to December 1990), White Plains, NY (December 1990 to March 1991), Pleasanton, CA (March 1991 to May 1993 and March 1994 to January 1998) and Point Reyes, CA (June 1993 to March 1994).

6.   I retired from AT&T in May 2004.

7.   AT&T Corp. (now a subsidiary of AT&T Inc.) maintains domestic telecommunications facilities over which millions of Americans' telephone and Internet communications pass every day. These facilities allow for the transmission of interstate or foreign electronic voice and data communications by the aid of wire, fiber optic cable, or other like connection between the point of origin and the point of reception.

8.   Between 1998 and 2003 I worked in an AT&T office located on Geary Street in San Francisco as one of six Computer Network Associates in the office. The site manager was a management-level technician with the title of Field Support Specialist (hereinafter referred to as FSS #1). Two other FSS people (FSS #2 and FSS #3) also operated from this

DECLARATION OF MARK KLEIN
C-06-0672-VRW

- 2 -

137

1 | office.

2 | 9.   During my service at the Geary Street facility, the office provided WorldNet
3 | Internet service, international and domestic Voice Over IP (voice communications
4 | transmitted over the Internet), and data transport service to the Asia/Pacific region.

5 | 10.   While I worked in the Geary Street facility in 2002, FSS #1 told me to expect a
6 | visit from a National Security Agency ("NSA") agent. I and other technicians also received
7 | an email from higher management advising us of the pending visit, and the email explicitly
8 | mentioned the NSA. FSS #1 told me the NSA agent was to interview FSS #2 for a special
9 | job. The NSA agent came and met with FSS #2. FSS #1 later confirmed to me that FSS #2
10 | was working on the special job, and that it was at the Folsom Street Facility.

11 | 11.   In January 2003, I, along with others, toured the Folsom Street Facility. The
12 | Folsom Street Facility consists of three floors of a building that was then operated by SBC
13 | Communications, Inc. (now known as AT&T Inc.).

14 | 12.   While on the January 2003 tour, I saw a new room being built adjacent to the
15 | 4ESS switch room. The new room was near completion. I saw a workman apparently
16 | working on the door lock for the room. I later learned that this new room being built was
17 | referred to in AT&T documents as the "SG3 Secure Room" (hereinafter the "SG3 Secure
18 | Room"). The SG3 Secure Room was room number 641A, and measures approximately 24
19 | by 48 feet.

20 | 13.   The 4ESS switch room is a room that contains a 4ESS switch, a type of
21 | electronic switching system that is used to direct long-distance telephone communications.
22 | AT&T uses the 4ESS switch in this room to route the public's telephone calls that transit
23 | through the Folsom Street Facility.

24 | 14.   FSS #2, the management-level technician whom the NSA cleared and
25 | approved for the special job referenced above, was the person working to install equipment
26 | in the SG3 Secure Room.

27 | 15.   In October 2003, the company transferred me to the AT&T Folsom Street
28 | Facility to oversee the WorldNet Internet room, as a Communications Technician.

APPENDIX B: DECLARATION

16.   In the Fall of 2003, FSS #1 told me that another NSA agent would again visit our office at Geary Street to talk to FSS #1 in order to get the latter's evaluation of FSS #3's suitability to perform the special job that FSS #2 had been doing. The NSA agent did come and speak to FSS #1. By January 2004, FSS #3 had taken over the special job as FSS #2 was forced to leave the company in a downsizing.

17.   The regular AT&T technician workforce was not allowed in the SG3 Secure Room. To my knowledge, only employees cleared by the NSA were permitted to enter the SG3 Secure Room. To gain entry to the SG3 Secure Room required both a physical key for the cylinder lock and a combination code number to be entered into an electronic keypad on the door. To my knowledge, only FSS #2, and later FSS #3, had both the key and the combination code. Regular technicians, including myself, had keys to every other door in the facility because we were often there working alone. We were not given either a key or the combination code for the SG3 Secure Room. On one occasion, when FSS #3 was retrieving a circuit card for me from the SG3 Secure Room, he invited me into the room with him for a couple of minutes while he retrieved the circuit card from a storage cabinet and showed me some poorly installed cable.

18.   The extremely limited access to the SG3 Secure Room was highlighted by one incident in 2003. FSS #1 told me that the large industrial air conditioner in the SG3 Secure Room was leaking water through the floor and onto SBC's equipment downstairs, but FSS #2 was not immediately available to provide servicing, and the regular technicians had no access, so the semi-emergency continued for some days until FSS #2 arrived.

19.   AT&T provides dial-up and DSL Internet services to its customers through its WorldNet service. The WorldNet Internet room included large routers, racks of modems for AT&T customers' WorldNet dial-in services, and other telecommunications equipment. The equipment in the WorldNet Internet room was used to direct emails, web browsing requests and other electronic communications sent to or from the customers of AT&T's WorldNet Internet service.

20.   In the course of my employment, I was responsible for troubleshooting

DECLARATION OF MARK KLEIN
C-06-0672-VRW
                                                                                    - 4 -

139

1   problems on the fiber optic circuits and installing new fiber optic circuits.

2   21.   The fiber optic cables used by AT&T typically consist of up to 96 optical
3   fibers, which are flexible thin glass fibers capable of transmitting communications through
4   light signals.

5   22.   Within the WorldNet Internet room, high speed fiber optic circuits connect to
6   routers for AT&T's WorldNet Internet service and are part of the AT&T WorldNet's
7   "Common Backbone" (CBB). The CBB comprises a number of major hub facilities, such as
8   the Folsom Street Facility, connected by a mesh of high-speed (OC3, OC12, OC48 and some
9   even higher speed) optical circuits.

10   23.   Unlike traditional copper wire circuits, which emit electromagnetic fields that
11   can be tapped into without disturbing the circuits, fiber optic circuits do not "leak" their light
12   signals. In order to monitor such communications, one has to physically cut into the fiber
13   and divert a portion of the light signal to access the information.

14   24.   A fiber optic circuit can be split using splitting equipment to divide the light
15   signal and to divert a portion of the signal into each of two fiber optic cables. While both
16   signals will have a reduced signal strength, after the split both signals still contain the same
17   information, effectively duplicating the communications that pass through the splitter.

18   25.   In the course of my employment, I reviewed two "Cut-In and Test Procedure"
19   documents dated January 13, 2003 and January 24, 2003, which instructed technicians on
20   how to connect the already in-service circuits to a "splitter cabinet," which diverted light
21   signals from the WorldNet Internet service's fiber optical circuits to the SG3 Secure Room.

22   26.   A true and correct copy of the "Cut-In and Test Procedure" documents are
23   attached hereto as Exhibits A and B. Exhibit A is the January 13, 2003 document, and
24   Exhibit B is the January 24, 2003 document.

25   27.   The light signals from the WorldNet Internet service's optical circuits were
26   split, with a portion of the light signal going through fiber optic cables into the SG3 Secure
27   Room. The AT&T location code of the "splitter cabinet" is 070177.04, which denotes the
28   7th floor, aisle 177 and bay 04.

DECLARATION OF MARK KLEIN
C-06-0672-VRW   - 5 -

1   28.   In the course of my employment, I reviewed a document entitled "Study Group

2 3, LGX/Splitter Wiring, San Francisco" dated December 10, 2002, authored by AT&T Labs'.

3 consultant Mathew F. Casamassima. A true and correct copy of this document is attached

4 hereto as Exhibit C. This document described the connections from the SG3 Secure Room

5 on the 6th floor to the WorldNet Internet room on the 7th floor, and provided diagrams on

6 how the light signal was being split.

7   29.   The circuits that were listed in the "Cut-in and Test Procedure" document

8 dated January 24, 2003 are "Peering Links" that connect the WorldNet Internet network to

9 national and international Internet networks of non-AT&T telecommunications companies.

10   30.   The "Cut-In and Test Procedure" documents provided procedures to "cut-in"

11 AT&T's Peering Links to the splitter and hence to the SG3 Secure Room.

12   31.   Starting in February 2003, the "splitter cabinet" split (and diverted to the SG3

13 Secure Room) the light signals that contained the communications in transit to and from

14 AT&T's Peering Links with the following Internet networks and Internet exchange points:

15 ConXion, Verio, XO, Genuity, Qwest, PAIX, Allegiance, Abovenet, Global Crossing, C&W,

16 UUNET, Level 3, Sprint, Telia, PSINet, and MAE-West.

17   32.   MAE-West is an Internet nodal point and one of the largest "Internet exchange

18 points" in the United States. PAIX, the Palo Alto Internet Exchange, is another significant

19 Internet exchange point.

20   33.   Internet exchange points are facilities at which large numbers of major Internet

21 service providers interconnect their equipment in order to facilitate the exchange of

22 communications among their respective networks.

23   34.   Through the "splitter cabinet," the content of all of the electronic voice and

24 data communications going across the Peering Links mentioned in paragraphs 29 to 31 was

25 transferred from the WorldNet Internet room's fiber optical circuits into the SG3 Secure

26 Room.

27   35.   The document "Study Group 3, LGX/Splitter Wiring, San Francisco" dated

28 December 10, 2002, listed the equipment installed in the SG3 Secure Room, including such

DECLARATION OF MARK KLEIN
C-06-0672-VRW

- 6 -

1   equipment as Sun servers and Juniper (M40e and M160) "backbone" routers. This list also

2   included a Narus STA 6400, which is a "Semantic Traffic Analyzer."

3   36.   In the course of my employment, I was required to connect new circuits to the

4   "splitter cabinet" and get them up and running. While working on a particularly difficult one

5   with another AT&T technician, I learned that other such "splitter cabinets" were being

6   installed in other cities, including Seattle, San Jose, Los Angeles and San Diego.

7

8   I declare under penalty of perjury under the laws of the United States that the

9   foregoing is true and correct.

10

11   DATED: March 28, 2006

12

13   /s/

                                                    Mark Klein

14

15

16

17

18

19

20

21

22

23

24

25

26

27

28

Appendix C

Amicus Curiae Brief of Mark Klein

May 4, 2006

Submitted by Mark Klein's attorneys James J. Brosnahan,
Tony West, Miles Ehrlich and Ismail Ramsey to the
U.S. District Court, Northern District of California,
Judge Vaughn Walker presiding, in the case of
Hepting v. AT&T

APPENDIX C: AMICUS BRIEF

1 JAMES J. BROSNAHAN (BAR NO. 34555)
   TONY WEST (BAR NO. 164151)
2 MORRISON & FOERSTER LLP
   425 Market Street
3 San Francisco, California 94105-2482
   Telephone: 415.268.7000
4 Facsimile: 415.268.7522
   JBrosnahan@mofo.com
5
   ISMAIL RAMSEY (BAR NO. 189820)
6 MILES EHRLICH (BAR NO. 237954)
   RAMSEY & EHRLICH LLP
7 803 Hearst Avenue
   Berkeley, CA 94710
8 Telephone: 510.548.3600
   Facsimile: 510.548.3601
9 miles@ramsey-ehrlich.com

10 Attorneys for MARK KLEIN

11   UNITED STATES DISTRICT COURT

12   NORTHERN DISTRICT OF CALIFORNIA

13   SAN FRANCISCO DIVISION

14

15 TASH HEPTING, GREGORY HICKS,   Case No. C-06-00672-VRW
   CAROLYN JEWEL and ERIK KNUTZEN
16 on Behalf of Themselves and All Others   **BRIEF OF AMICUS CURIAE**
   Similarly Situated,,   **MARK KLEIN**
17
                  Plaintiff,
18
         v.
19   Hearing Date: N/A
   AT&T CORP., AT&T INC. and DOES 1-   Time: N/A
20 20, inclusive,   Courtroom: 6 (17th floor)
                                           Judge: Hon. Vaughn Walker
21   Defendant.

22

23

24

25

26

27

28

BRIEF OF AMICUS CURIAE MARK KLEIN
C-06-00672-VRW
sf-2122400

144

APPENDIX C: AMICUS BRIEF

I.   **INTRODUCTION**

This amicus brief addresses a limited issue before the Court: Whether Mark Klein's declaration, now temporarily lodged under seal, should be unsealed and filed in the public record. Because the substance of Mr. Klein's declaration is based on his observations which corroborate publicly-available information and Mr. Klein's voice is an important, informed addition to the public debate about the legality of the government's wiretapping program, Mr. Klein urges this Court to unseal his declaration.

II.   **MARK KLEIN'S INTEREST IN THE CASE.**

Mr. Klein is not a party to these proceedings. He has no economic stake in the outcome of this case. For 22 years, Mr. Klein worked for AT&T. A member of the Communications Workers of America, every personnel review in Mr. Klein's file rated his performance as "outstanding" or "more than satisfactory" during that time. Mr. Klein is now a retiree.

Mr. Klein is also a witness. During the last year he worked for AT&T, Mr. Klein observed governmental activity that he believes violates the Constitution and laws of the United States. What he learned about the government's wiretapping program Mr. Klein learned in the course of performing his duties for AT&T. At no time did anyone tell Mr. Klein — neither the government nor anyone else — that the things he observed while doing his job were "top secret," "classified," or otherwise regarded as a "state secret." In fact, when materials attached in support of Mr. Klein's declaration were forwarded by the plaintiffs to the Department of Justice for review, the government responded that it did not object to the documents being filed under seal.

There is presently an important public debate on the legality of NSA's wiretapping program. That debate started before any participation by Mr. Klein. More important this court must decide certain issues relating to that program. Some materials that Mr. Klein gave to the plaintiffs in this case the plaintiff then voluntarily sent to the Department of Justice to the attention of an appropriate person. The government representative had the materials for no fewer than four days, plenty of time to consult with all necessary persons

145

1 within the government. That person then advised the plaintiffs that they could be filed in

2 court. After the government was asked about the materials being filed and after the

3 government approved them for filing the government did not claim they were classified or

4 a state secret. In summery the government has never treated Mr. Klein's knowledge or

5 materials as classified or as government secrets. The government has at no time attempted

6 to put Mr. Klein's materials, or treat his information as classified or as a government secret

7 by insisting that it be put, in a sensitive compartmented information facility ("SCIF").

8 Sensitive national security information is classified and safeguarded according to

9 established procedures. *See* 60 Fed. Reg. 19825 (1995). The government never did that.

10 On the contrary, after conducting a thorough review, the Department of Justice chose not to

11 classify the documents at issue and expressly authorized the plaintiffs to file the material in

12 this Court (albeit it was to be under seal). For all these years the government has treated

13 what Mr. Klein knows and his materials as not worthy of classification or state secret

14 designation. The other party now attempting to keep the public from knowing what they

15 have done, AT&T, never advised Mr. Klein that his knowledge or materials should be

16 treated as classified or as state secrets.

17 **III.   THE TECHNOLOGY MARK KLEIN OBSERVED IS PUBLIC INFORMATION.**

18   Mark Klein's declaration is based on his personal observations and is relevant to a

19 robust, national debate currently taking place around the country. As an AT&T technician,

20 Mr. Klein's job included repairing and maintaining the fiber optic cables that carry Internet

21 data from all over the world through AT&T's San Francisco central switch. What he

22 observed — that the signal carrying the Internet data over fiber optic cables was "split"

23 such that an exact copy of the data was redirected to the National Security Agency

24 ("NSA") — had been the topic of public discussion months before he went public with his

25 observations.

26   For example, on December 22, 2005, CNET News.com posed the question, "Just

27 how extensive is NSA's spy program?" Declan McCullagh, "Just How Extensive is NSA's

28 Spy Program," December 22, 2005, available at (http://news.com.com/Just+how+

APPENDIX C: AMICUS BRIEF

1   extensive+is+NSAs+spy+program/2100-1028_3-6006326.html). CNET reported that

2   despite the Administration's forceful defense of the program,

3   some technologists and civil libertarians, using clues that dribbled
out in press briefings and news articles, are concluding that the

4   operation involves widespread monitoring of millions of e-mail
messages and telephone conversations that cross any U.S. border.

5

6   *Id.* In fact, reported CNET, "'[t]he clues are piling up that *vacuum-cleaner style dragnets are*

7   *what's at issue*,' John Gilmore, co-founder of the Electronic Frontier Foundation, said in a

8   mailing list message on Thursday." *Id.* (emphasis added).

9   Two days after CNET News.com published its story, on December 24, 2005, Reuters

10   headlined: "NSA spy program broader than Bush admitted." Reuters, "NSA Spy Program

11   Broader than Bush Admitted," December 24, 2005, available at http://www.msnbc.msn.com/id/

12   10592932/ (emphasis added). The Reuters report was based on an earlier *New York Times* article

13   which cited "current and former government officials" who said that "information was collected

14   [without warrants by the NSA] by tapping directly into some of the U.S. telecommunication

15   system's main arteries." *Id.*

16   In addition, on January 10, ABC News reported that, according to NSA whistleblower

17   Russell Tice, the NSA program "may have involved spying on millions of Americans, not just a

18   few highly suspicious characters." Brian Ross, "NSA Insider Speaks Out," January 10, 2006,

19   available at http://abcnews.go.com/Nightline/story?id=1860899&page=1. In a televised

20   interview, Tice admitted to being one of the sources the *New York Times* used when it broke the

21   story about the NSA's eavesdropping program in early December 2005. Importantly, when asked

22   whether he had revealed any classified information to the *Times,* Tice responded: "No. No. I've

23   not told them anything classified." *Id.*

24   Joining the major news media's chorus were groups like the American Civil Liberties

25   Union ("ACLU"), who, on January 31, 2006, posted on their website that the "NSA has gained

26   direct access to the telecommunications infrastructure through some of America's largest

27   companies." American Civil Liberties Union, "Eavesdropping 101: What can the NSA Do?"

28   available at http://www.aclu.org/safefree/nsaspying/23989res20060131.html. Without any help

147

1 from Mr. Klein, the ACLU went on to detail a "major new element of the NSA's spying

2 machinery is its ability to tap directly into the major communications switches, routing stations,

3 or access points of the telecommunications system." The ACLU noted that by working with

4 leading telecommunications companies, the NSA has obtained a "new level of direct access" to

5 the nation's telecommunications infrastructure that "apparently includes both some of the

6 gateways through which phone calls are routed, as well as other key nodes through which a large

7 proportion of Internet traffic passes." And "most significantly," reported the ACLU, "access to

8 these 'switches' and other network hubs give the agency access to a direct feed of all the

9 communications that pass through them, and the ability to filter, sift through, analyze, read, or

10 share those communications as it sees fit." *Id.*

11   The ACLU also directed users to a map entitled, "Eavesdropping 101: What Can the

12 NSA Do?" which purported to show how the NSA "has extended its tentacles into much of the

13 U.S. civilian communications infrastructure, including, it appears, the 'switches' through which

14 international and some domestic communications are routed, Internet exchange points, individual

15 telephone company central facilities, and Internet Service Providers (ISPs)." *Id.* (A true and

16 correct copy of the ACLU's map is attached hereto as Exhibit A.)

17   Far from releasing any new information or "state secret," Mr. Klein's observations

18 corroborate opinions that have been voiced in a public debate that has been raging long before

19 Mr. Klein came forward. Mr. Klein's participation in this public discussion is important because

20 his is a viewpoint informed by first-hand observations and bolstered by decades of technical

21 expertise. Indeed, by coming forward, Mr. Klein has engaged in the very type of national

22 conversation Senator Arlen Specter (R-PA) encouraged when he said earlier this year that he

23 hoped "public concern and public indignation [would] build up" such that that scrutiny of the

24 Administration's eavesdropping program does not wane. Declan McCullagh, "NSA Spying

25 Come Under Legal, Political Attack," April 28, 2006, available at http://news.com.com/NSA+

26 spying+comes+under+legal%2C+political+attack/2100-1028_3-6066123.html.

27   Mr. Klein's declaration and the information it relates regards information about publicly-

28 known and publicly-discussed technology. His observations corroborate his belief and the

APPENDIX C: AMICUS BRIEF

1 opinions of others that the government has obtained access to all e-mails, telephone calls and web

2 browsing that go through the AT&T facility. Mr. Klein believes this government access is an

3 illegal interception of domestic wire communications prohibited by the Electronic

4 Communications Privacy Act, 18 U.S.C. 2511, *et seq.*, Foreign Intelligence Surveillance Act,

5 50 U.S.C. 1801, *et seq.*

6   Mr. Klein also believes that this government access is unconstitutional if no warrant has

7 been obtained to justify the access as required by the Fourth Amendment of the U.S. Constitution,

8 as appears to be the case from recent statements by Members of Congress. *See* U.S. Const.

9 Amend. IV ("The right of the people to be secure in their persons, houses, papers, and effects

10 against unreasonable searches and seizures, shall not be violated, and no Warrants shall issue, but

11 upon probable cause, supported by Oath or affirmation, and particularly describing the place to be

12 searched, and the persons to be seized.")

13 **IV.   LIMITED REQUEST FROM MR. KLEIN.**

14   Mr. Klein asks that his declaration be unsealed.

15

16 Dated: May 4, 2006   Respectfully submitted,

17   JAMES J. BROSNAHAN
                                                   TONY WEST
18   MORRISON & FOERSTER LLP

19

20   By: _____/s/_____
21   James J. Brosnahan
                                                       Attorneys for MARK KLEIN
22

23   ISMAIL RAMSEY
                                                   MILES EHRLICH
24   RAMSEY & EHRLICH LLP

25

26   By: _____/s/_____
                                                       Ismail Ramsey
27   Attorneys for MARK KLEIN

28

149

Exhibit A

EAVESDROPPING 101:
WHAT CAN THE NSA DO?

The recent revelations about illegal eavesdropping on American citizens by the U.S. National Security Agency have raised many questions about just what the agency is doing. Although the facts are just beginning to emerge, information that has come to light about the NSA's activities and capabilities over the years, as well as the recent reporting by the *New York Times* and others, allows us to discern the outlines of what they are likely doing and how they are doing it.

The NSA is not only the world's largest spy agency (far larger than the CIA, for example), but it possesses the most advanced technology for intercepting communications. We know it has long had the ability to focus powerful surveillance capabilities on particular individuals or communications. But the current scandal has indicated two new and significant elements of the agency's eavesdropping:

The NSA has gained direct access to the telecommunications infrastructure through some of America's largest companies The agency appears to be not only targeting individuals, but also using broad "data mining" systems that allow them to intercept and evaluate the communications of millions of people within the United States.

The ACLU has prepared a map [see page 2] illustrating how all this is believed to work. It shows how the military spying agency has extended its tentacles into much of the U.S. civilian communications infrastructure, including, it appears, the "switches" through which international and some domestic communications are routed, Internet exchange points, individual telephone company central facilities, and Internet Service Providers (ISP). While we cannot be certain about these secretive links, this chart shows a representation of what is, according to recent reports, the most likely picture of what is going on.

CORPORATE BEDFELLOWS
One major new element of the NSA's spying machinery is its ability to tap directly into the major communications switches, routing stations, or access points of the telecommunications system. For example, according to the *New York Times*, the NSA has worked with "the leading companies" in the telecommunications industry to collect communications patterns, and has gained access "to switches

that act as gateways" at "some of the main arteries for moving voice and some Internet traffic into and out of the United States."[1]

This new level of direct access apparently includes both some of the gateways through which phone calls are routed, as well as other key nodes through which a large proportion of Internet traffic passes. This new program also recognizes that today's voice and Internet communications systems are increasingly converging, with a rising proportion of even voice phone calls moving to the Internet via VOIP, and parts of the old telephone transmission system being converted to fiber optic cable and used for both data and voice communications. While data and voice sometimes travel together and sometimes do not, and we do not know exactly which "switches" and other access points the NSA has tapped, what appears certain is that the NSA is looking at both.

And most significantly, access to these "switches" and other network hubs give the agency access to a direct feed of all the communications that pass through them, and the ability to filter, sift through, analyze, read, or share those communications as it sees fit.

DATA MINING
The other major novelty in the NSA's activities appears to be the exploitation of a new concept in surveillance that has attracted a lot of attention in the past few years: what is commonly called "data mining." Unlike the agency's longstanding practice of spying on specific individuals and communications based upon some source of suspicion, data mining involves formula-based searches through mountains of data for individuals whose behavior or profile is in some way suspiciously different from the norm.

Data mining is a broad dragnet. Instead of targeting you because you once received a telephone call from a person who received a telephone call from a person who is a suspected terrorist, you might be targeted because the NSA's computers have analyzed your communications and have determined that they contain certain words or word combinations, addressing information, or other factors with a frequency that deviates from the average, and which they have decided might be an indication of suspiciousness. The

NSA has no prior reason to suspect you, and you are in no way tied to any other suspicious individuals – you have just been plucked out of the crowd by a computer algorithm's analysis of your behavior.

Use of these statistical fishing expeditions has been made possible by the access to communications streams granted by key corporations. The NSA may also be engaging in "geographic targeting," in which they listen in on communications between the United States and a particular foreign country or region. More broadly, data mining has been greatly facilitated by underlying changes in technology that have taken place in the past few years [see page 3].

This dragnet approach is not only bad for civil liberties – it is also a bad use of our scarce security and law enforcement resources. In fact, the creation of large numbers of wasteful and distracting leads is one of the primary reasons that many security experts say data mining and other dragnet strategies are a poor way of preventing crime and terrorism. The *New York Times* confirmed that point, with its report that the NSA has sent the FBI a "flood" of tips generated by mass domestic eavesdropping and data mining, virtually all of which led to dead ends that wasted the FBI's resources. "We'd chase a number, find it's a schoolteacher with no indication they've ever been involved in international terrorism," one former FBI agent told the *Times*. "After you get a thousand numbers and not one is turning up anything, you get some frustration."[2]

COMBINING TELECOMMUNICATIONS AND OTHER PRIVATE DATA?
The NSA has historically been in the business of intercepting and analyzing communications data. One question is whether or not this communications data is being combined with other intimate details about our lives. A few years ago, the Pentagon began work on an breathtaking data mining program called Total Information Awareness, which envisioned programming computers to trawl through an extensive list of information on Americans (including, according to the program's own materials, "Financial, Education, Travel, Medical, Veterinary, Country Entry, Place/Event Entry, Transportation, Housing, Critical Resources, Government, Communications") in the hunt for "suspicious" patterns of activity. Congress decisively

APPENDIX C: AMICUS BRIEF

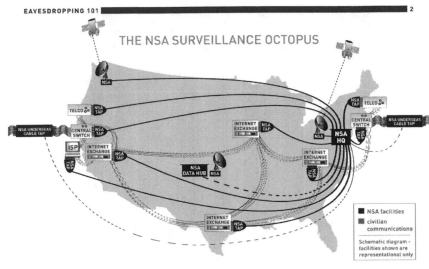

THE NSA SURVEILLANCE OCTOPUS

■ NSA facilities
■ civilian communications

Schematic diagram - facilities shown are representational only

 Yakima listening post One way that telephone calls and other communications are sent from the United States to Asia and other destinations is via satellite and microwave transmissions. This NSA satellite facility on a restricted Army firing range in Yakima, Washington sweeps in millions of communications an hour from international communications satellites.

 Sugar Grove listening post One way that telephone calls and other communications are sent from the United States to Europe and other destinations is via satellite and microwave transmissions. This NSA satellite facility, located in an isolated valley in Sugar Grove, West Virginia, sweeps in millions of communications an hour from international communications satellites.

 Internet Service Provider (ISP) The NSA may be forcing ISPs to provide it with information in the form of a computer tap (similar to a controversial FBI device dubbed "Carnivore") that scans all the communications that reach that ISP.

 Central switch These facilities, one in New York and one in Northern California, are operated by major telecommunications companies. They are a primary means by which a mix of voice and data communications, including those that travel over transoceanic undersea fiber optic cables, are routed ("switched") toward their proper destination. Because they serve as central switching points, they offer the NSA access to a large volume of communications.

 Internet exchange These publicly or privately owned "Internet exchanges" are where Internet traffic is exchanged between the sub-networks that make up the Internet. These public or privately owned facilities are divided into Tier 1, Tier 2, and Tier 3 exchanges. The Tier 1 exchanges, typically located in big cities, are the ones that have national and global reach and are likely to be of most interest to the NSA.

 Underseas cable tap According to published reports, American divers were able to install surveillance devices onto the transoceanic cables that carry phone calls and data across the seas. One of these taps was discovered in 1982, but other devices apparently continued to function undetected. The advent of fiber-optic cables posed challenges for the NSA, but there is no reason to believe that that problem remained unsolved by the agency.

 The NSA's headquarters Tens of thousands of people, including intelligence analysts, linguists and computer professionals, work at this complex in Fort Meade, Maryland outside of Washington, DC. NSA headquarters is where the millions of intercepted communications are processed and analyzed.

 Telco: Domestic telephone company The NSA is apparently hooking in to U.S. telephone companies, which have not only networks that can be tapped into, but also records of customer communications.

 NSA Data Hub: Domestic Warning Hub and Data Warehouse, Aurora, CO The NSA is reportedly building a massive data storage facility in this Denver suburb, and also operates a reconaissance satellite dish here. This may be where the agency's data mining operations take place. A CIA facility and the military's Northern Command (NORTHCOM) are also located here.

rejected this approach, voting to shut down the program, at least for domestic use – but we know Congress allowed elements of the program to be moved undercover, into the bowels of the Pentagon, while supposedly being restricted to non-Americans. We also know that the NSA is sharing its information with other security services. What we do not know is whether any of information from TIA-like enterprises is being combined with the NSA's communications intercepts.

HOW THE NSA SEARCHES FOR TARGETS

There are a range of techniques that are probably used by the NSA to sift through the sea of communications it steals from the world's cables and airwaves:

Keywords. In this longstanding technique, the agency maintains a watch list or "dictionary" of key words, individuals, telephone numbers and presumably now computer IP addresses. It uses that list to pick out potentially relevant communications from all the data that it gathers. These keywords are often provided to the NSA by other security agencies, and the NSA passes the resulting intelligence "take" back to the other agencies or officials. According to the law, the NSA must strip out the names and other identifying information of Americans captured inadvertently, a process called "minimization." (According to published reports, those minimization procedures are not being properly observed.) In the 1990s, it was revealed that the NSA had used the word "Greenpeace" and "Amnesty" (as in the human rights group Amnesty International) as keywords as part of its "Echelon" program (see below).

Link analysis. It is believed that another manner in which individuals are now being added to the watch lists is through a process often called "link analysis." Link analysis can work like this: the CIA captures a terrorist's computer on the battlefield and finds a list of phone numbers, including some U.S. numbers. The NSA puts those numbers on their watch list. They add the people that are called from those numbers to their list. They could then in turn add the people called from *those* numbers to their list. How far they carry that process and what standards if any govern the process is unknown.

Other screening techniques. There may be other techniques that the NSA could be using to pluck out potential targets. One example is voice pattern analysis, in which computers listen for the sound of, say, Osama Bin Laden's voice. No one knows how accurate

the NSA's computers may be at such tasks, but if commercial attempts at analogous activities such as face recognition are any guide, they would also be likely to generate enormous numbers of false hits.

A THREE-STAGE PROCESS

So how are all these new techniques and capabilities being put into practice? Presumably, "The Program" (as insiders reportedly refer to the illegal practices) continues to employ watch lists and dictionaries. We do not know how the newer and more sophisticated link analysis and statistical data mining techniques are being used.

But, a good guess is that the NSA is following a three-stage process for the broadest portion of its sweep through the communications infrastructure:

1. The Dragnet: a search for targets. In this stage, the NSA sifts through the data coursing through the arteries of our telecom systems, making use of such factors as keyword searches, telephone number and IP address targeting, and techniques such as link analysis, and "data mining." At this stage, the communications of millions of people may be scrutinized.

2. Human review: making the target list. Communications and individuals that are flagged by the system for one reason or another are presumably then subject to human review. An analyst looks at the origin, destination and content of the communication and makes a determination as to whether further eavesdropping or investigation is desired. We have absolutely no idea what kind of numbers are involved at this stage.

3. The Microscope: targeting listed individuals. Finally, individuals determined to be suspicious in phase two are presumably placed on a target list so that they are placed under the full scrutiny of the NSA's giant surveillance microscope, with all their communications captured and analyzed.

EXPANDING SURVEILLANCE AS TECHNOLOGY CHANGES

Today's NSA spying is a response to, and has been made possible by, some of the fundamental technological changes that have taken place in recent years. Around the end of 1990s, the NSA began to complain privately – and occasionally publicly – that they were being overrun by technology as communications increasingly went digital. One change in particular was especially significant: electronic communications ranging from email to

voice conversations were increasingly using the new and different protocols of the Internet.

The consequence of this change was that the NSA felt it was forced to change the points in the communications infrastructure that it targeted – but having done that, it gained the ability to analyze vastly more and richer communications.

The Internet and technologies that rely upon it (such as electronic mail, web surfing and Internet-based telephones known as Voice over IP or VOIP) works by breaking information into small "packets." Each packet is then routed across the network of computers that make up the Internet according to the most efficient path at that moment, like a driver trying to avoid traffic jams as he makes his way across a city. Once all the packets – which are labeled with their origin, destination and other "header" information – have arrived, they are then reassembled.

An important result of this technology is that on the Internet, there is no longer a meaningful distinction between "domestic" and "international" routes of a communication. It was once relatively easy for the NSA, which by law is limited to "foreign intelligence," to aim its interception technologies at purely "foreign" communications. But now, an e-mail sent from London to Paris, for example, might well be routed through the west coast of the United States (when, for example, it is a busy mid-morning in Europe but the middle of the night in California) along the same path traveled by mail between Los Angeles and San Francisco.

That system makes the NSA all the more eager to get access to centralized Internet exchange points operated by a few telecommunications giants. But because of the way this technology works, eavesdropping on an IP communication is a completely different ballgame from using an old-fashioned "wiretap" on a single line. The packets of interest to the eavesdropper are mixed in with all the other traffic that crosses through that pathway – domestic and international.

ECHELON

Much of what we know about the NSA's spying prior to the recent revelations comes from the late 1990s, when a fair amount of information emerged about a system popularly referred to by the name "Echelon" – a code-name the NSA had used at least one time (although their continued use of the term, if at all, is unknown). Echelon was a system for mass eavesdropping on communications around the world by the NSA and its allies

APPENDIX C: AMICUS BRIEF

nong the intelligence agencies of other
itions. The best source of information on
helon was two reports commissioned by
e European Parliament (in part due to suspi-
ns among Europeans that the NSA was car-
ing out economic espionage on behalf of
nerican corporations). Other bits of informa-
n were gleaned from documents obtained
rough the U.S. Freedom of Information Act,
well as statements by foreign governments
at were partners in the program (the UK,
ıstralia, Canada, and New Zealand).

s of the late 1990s/early 2000s, Echelon
vept up global communications using two
imary methods:

The interception of satellite and microwave
gnals. One way that telephone calls and
her communications are sent from the
ited States to Europe and other destina-
ns is via satellite and microwave transmis-
ns. ECHELON was known to use
imerous satellite receivers ("dishes") –
cated on the east and west coasts of the
ited States, in England, Australia,
ırmany, and elsewhere around the globe –
vacuum up the "spillover" broadcasts from
ese satellite transmissions.

Transoceanic cable tapping. ECHELON's
her primary eavesdropping method was to
p into the transoceanic cables that also
ırry phone calls across the seas. According
published reports, American divers were
le to install surveillance devices onto these
ıbles. One of these taps was discovered in
'82, but other devices apparently continued
function undetected. It is more difficult to
p into fiber-optic cables (which unlike other
ıbles do not "leak" radio signals that can be
cked up by a device attached to the outside
the cable), but there is no reason to believe
at that problem remained unsolved by the
jency.

e do not know the extent to which these
ources of data continue to be significant for
e NSA, or the extent to which they have
en superseded by the agency's new direct
:cess to the infrastructure, including the
ternet itself, over which both voice and data
mmunications travel.

NANSWERED QUESTIONS

ıe bottom line is that the NSA appears to be
ıpable not only of intercepting the interna-
ınal communications of a relatively small
ımber of targeted Americans, but also of
tercepting a sweeping amount of U.S. com-
unications (through corporate-granted
:cess to communications "pipes" and

"boxes"), and of performing mass analysis on
those communications (through data mining
and other techniques).

Despite the fuzzy picture of "The Program"
that we now possess, the current spying
scandal has highlighted many unanswered
questions about the NSA's current activities.
They include:

- Just what kinds of communications
  arteries has the NSA tapped into?

- What kinds of filters or analysis is the NSA
  applying to the data that flows through
  those arteries? How are data mining and
  other new techniques being used?

- Which telecom providers are cooperating
  with the NSA?

- How are subjects selected for targeted
  intercepts?

- What kinds of information exchange are
  taking place between the NSA and other
  security agencies? We know they probably
  turn over to other agencies any data turned
  up by watch list entries submitted by those
  other agencies, and they are also
  apparently passing along data
  mining-generated "cold hits" to the FBI
  and perhaps other security agencies for
  further investigation. Does information
  flow the other way as well – are other
  agencies giving data to the NSA for help in
  that second phase of deciding who gets put
  under the microscope?

- Is data that NSA collects, under whatever
  rubric, being merged with other data,
  either by NSA or another agency? Is
  communications data being merged with
  other transactional information, such as
  credit card, travel, and financial data, in the
  fashion of the infamous "Total Information
  Awareness" data mining program? (TIA,
  while prohibited by Congress from engaging
  in "domestic" activities, still exists within the
  Pentagon – and can be used for "foreign
  intelligence purposes.) Just how many
  schoolteachers and other innocent
  Americans have been investigated as a
  result of "The Program?" And just how
  much privacy invasion are they subject to
  before the FBI can conclude they are not
  "involved in international terrorism"?

Rarely if ever in American history has a government agency possessed so much power
subject to so little oversight. Given that situation, abuses were inevitable – and any limits

to those abuses a matter of mere good fortune.
If our generation of leaders and citizens does
not rise to the occasion, we will prove ourselves
to be unworthy of the heritage that we have
been so fortunate to inherit from our Founders.

ENDNOTES

[1] Eric Lichtblau and James Risen, "Spy
Agency Mined Vast Data Trove, Officials
Report," New York Times, December 24,
2005;
http://select.nytimes.com/search/restricted/
article?res=FA0714F63E540C778EDDAB0994
DD404482

[2] Lowell Bergman, Eric Lichtblau, Scott Shane
and Don Van Natta Jr., "Spy Agency Data After
Sept. 11 Led F.B.I. to Dead Ends," New York
Times, January 17, 2006;
http://www.nytimes.com/2006/01/17/poli-
tics/17spy.html.

Index

INDEX

Internet Resources

For those who want to do further research on this story, the following list of key material through June 2009 provides some good starting points, although it is by no means exhaustive. Google for the exact web addresses.

Electronic Frontier Foundation *eff.org*
EFF's excellent site provides the actual legal documents in the court battles, and ongoing news about civil liberties.

Wired.com was the first to reveal the AT&T documents and has closely followed the NSA story.

ABC Nightline with Brian Ross, Mar. 6, 2007 *abcnews.com*
The title of the text story is "Whistle-blower Had to Fight NSA, LA Times to Tell Story," and video is included

PBS Frontline, "Spying on the Home Front," May 15, 2007 *pbs.org*
Excellent five-part show with veteran correspondent Hedrick Smith. Part 3 is "The NSA's Eavesdropping at AT&T."

MSNBC Countdown with Keith Olbermann *msn.com*
"Whistleblower saw AT&T assist Bush administration," Nov. 7, 2007 (Posted on YouTube)

NPR *All Things Considered* with Robert Siegel *npr.org*
"AT&T Wiretap Whistleblower Fights Senate Deal," Nov. 7, 2007

Senator Chris Dodd:
1. Staff interview with Mark Klein, Nov. 7, 2007 (Posted on YouTube)
2. Speech on the Senate floor, Dec. 17, 2007 *C-Span.org*
Dodd's long speech was part of his filibuster against immunity for the telecoms, and he read lengthy excerpts from technical documents of Mark Klein into the Congressional record. (Posted on YouTube)

Democracy Now! with Amy Goodman *democracynow.org*
"AT&T Whistleblower Urges Against Immunity for Telecoms in Bush Spy Program," July 7, 2008

Contact

Bookstores can order this book from:
BookSurge
Baker & Taylor

Media can contact Mark Klein at
markklein2009@gmail.com

sites.google.com/site/markklein2009

About the Author

MARK KLEIN is the whistleblower who exposed AT&T's participation in the National Security Agency's illegal warrantless spying on millions of Americans.

Klein grew up in New York City and in 1962 entered Cornell University's School of Engineering. As the 1960s exploded in social upheaval he was moved with his generation to investigate society and graduated in 1966 with a B.A. in history. Later he returned to technical school, obtaining certificates in electronics and computers which led to employment in computer manufacturing in the 1970s.

He was hired by AT&T in 1981 as a communications technician and worked for the company for over 22 years. In 2003 he discovered the illicit NSA installation in San Francisco and three years later brought it to public attention. He retired from AT&T in May 2004, and now lives in the San Francisco Bay Area with his wife.

10413537R00093

Made in the USA
Charleston, SC
02 December 2011